Quinceañera!

Quinceañera!

The Essential Guide to
Planning the Perfect
Sweet Fifteen
Celebration

MICHELE SALCEDO

Henry Holt and Company / New York

Henry Holt and Company, Inc.
Publishers since 1866
115 West 18th Street
New York, New York 10011

Henry Holt® is a registered trademark
of Henry Holt and Company, Inc.

Published in Canada by Fitzhenry & Whiteside Ltd.,
195 Allstate Parkway, Markham, Ontario L3R 4T8.

Library of Congress Cataloging-in-Publication Data
Salcedo, Michele.
Quinceañera!: the essential guide to planning the perfect
sweet fifteen celebration / Michele Salcedo.—1st ed.
p.   cm.
Includes bibliographical references and index.
ISBN 0-8050-4465-5 (alk. paper)
I. Quinceañera (Social custom)—United States. I. Title.
GT2490.S25   1997   97-11893
395.2'4—dc21   CIP

Henry Holt books are available for special promotions
and premiums. For details contact: Director, Special Markets.

First Edition 1997

Designed by Michelle McMillian

FRONTISPIECE: *Maria Antonietta Castro* quinceañera. —Don Polo Video and Photo

Printed in the United States of America
All first editions are printed on acid-free paper. ∞

1   3   5   7   9   10   8   6   4   2

To my grandparents
Teodora Carmen Gutierrez Salcedo
and Gabriel Sainz Salcedo,
with whom I celebrated my quince años,
and to my father,
Ruben Paul Salcedo,
whose courage and perseverance taught me
the only insurmountable barriers are those we build

Contents ❧

Acknowledgments ❦

Quinceañeras celebrate a passage from one stage of life to the next in a strict sense, but they are so much more. At their best, they celebrate and renew family, strengthen the community, and instill pride in our respective cultures. During the year I've worked on this project, businessmen and -women, clergy, laity, and academics have opened their doors and given generously of their limited time and shared their vast knowledge. I would especially like to thank Concepción Aguilar, Elizabeth Arena, Susan Birkelo, Arturo Cortes, Nivaldo Cruz, Charles Dahm, Tomas de San Julian, Joe Duncan, Susan Eleutario, America Garcia, Rosemary Garcia, Rosario Garcia, Laura Guder, Lizy Hernandez, Tony and Frank Rodriguez, Fidel Hombra, Marilyn Galloway Lange, José López, Margarita Lopez, Francisco Macías and the staff at San Fernando Cathedral in San Antonio, Ramiro Matos, Ramón Menchaca, Cenaida Mendez, Ruth Mercado, Elma Muñiz, Juan Muñoz, Kathleen Murphy, Estersita and Aurelio Nodarse, José Luis Ovalle, Carlos Padrino, Arturo Perez, Rosendo Ramon, Maria Ramos, Hank Roa, Gloria Rodriguez, Juan D. Salinas III, Elias Sanchez, Joe Sanchez, Diana Sandoval, Emily Sokalov, Darlene and Andres Trujillo, Sister M. Theresa, Manuel Vasquez, and Juana Villavicencio.

This book would not have happened without the support of my agents, Barbara Lowenstein and Madeleine Morel, or my editors, Theresa Burns and Tracy Sherrod.

Amy Rosenthal was integral from begining to end. A very special thank-you goes to Evelyn Renold, for her support throughout the years. My editors at *Newsday*—Miriam Pawel, Bob Keane, and Tony Marro—generously gave me the time off to pursue this project. Thank you.

My friends were a tremendous source of support throughout this year. Special thanks go to Lea Llambelis, Ana Marengo, Maite Junco, Mireya Navarro, Michaele and David Haynes, Joanne Wells, Ramiro Burr, Jody and Bobby Kniejski, Paul and David Elizondo, Craig Thomason and Raul Rivera at the *San Antonio Express News,* Sheila Cullen, Edna Negrón, Octavio Nuiry, Fran McMorris, Dick Yarwood, Philip Ramos, Richard Haro, and especially Patty Hurtado and John Gierasch.

Margaret Denk, *mi hermana del corazón,* has done yeowoman's duty as photo researcher, which is such a small title for an enormous job. Danielle Duran ably helped with research. A very special thank-you goes to all the photographers who generously allowed me to publish their work. I am especially indebted to Beatriz Bernalde Casteñeda and to Carlos Reyes and his family and Graciela Rodriguez for lending me, a total stranger, photos from their family albums.

My family, I hold in my heart. My mother, Diane Rzany Salcedo, has been a lifelong example of incomparable courage, intellectual curiosity, and *corazón.* I am also grateful to my aunt and uncle, Phyllis and Arnold Salcedo, for their help on this project.

To the *quinceañeras* and their families I am greatly indebted. They invited me to their celebrations and into their homes, and then sat for hours patiently answering what must have seemed like the most insignificant questions during the interviews. Without the generous help of Blanca Argueta; Leonor Alvarez; Celia, Valentin, and Sylvia Hernandez; Sherry and Claudia Blend; Tomás and María Salazar; Rita Aguirre; Benita and Sarah Arevalo; Teresita and Ileana Perez; Nadia and Myra Ali; Lissette, Hazel, and Gilberto Cruz; Michele, Esther, and Rolando Nieto; Jacqueline, George, and Maria Delao; Norma Garcia; Lisa, Graciela, and Leslie Alfaro; Fanny, Concepcion, and María Padilla; Leticia and Maria Magaña; Marisela, Susana, and Angel Martinez; Amneris and Nereida Peña; AnnaMaria, Jayne, and David Padilla; Dominique Chavez; Rosario Cepín; Katia Roberno; Elena Romero; Ana Maria and Laura Valenzuela; and Enit Negrón, this book would not exist.

Introduction ❧

When girls are fifteen years old it is hard to distinguish if they are still in their childhood or if they are grown-up women. . . . They look like a blossom turning into flower. —Luz Solorio

High heels and lipstick. A beautiful ball gown. The dreamy rhythm of a waltz. A bejeweled crown sparkles in the spotlight as a proud father whirls his fifteen-year-old daughter out of childhood and into adolescence. Her family and friends applaud; her mother dabs a handkerchief to her eye. Life that night is a fairy tale, with ladies and chamberlains in attendance. She is a real-life princess—*la quinceañera.*

Today the quinceañera is a day and night of fantasy, but its roots go deep into Latin American cultural history. No less than Carlota, the Austrian empress of Mexico, and the Duchess of Alba are credited with cultivating rites of social passage to signal to everyone a more mature phase in a girl's life. But the beginnings go much further back, thousands of years back, to the indigenous people of our respective cultures. The Tainos and Arawaks, the Quechua and Toltecs, the Aztecs and Mayas, to name but a few—all had rites of passage to mark the point in a child's life when she was a child no longer, but ready to make her contribution to society as an adult. The preparations often took months and were marked with not only a community celebration but a spiritual celebration as well, as many Latinas celebrate their *quince años* today.

Some girls begin dreaming and planning their celebrations after going to an older sister's or cousin's event. Perhaps they are asked to stand in a court of honor. Or maybe a grandmother insists her granddaughter have one to keep or to start a family tradition or to celebrate her culture. In some communities, private clubs or religious auxiliaries sponsor what are called cotillions in Chicago and debuts in Puerto Rico and El Paso, Texas, but are nothing more or nothing less than one quinceañera for a group of girls.

Having a party is only one of several ways for the adults in one's family to acknowledge that a girl is becoming a woman. But one way or another, the passage is marked. The parents may offer their daughter a trip abroad, a car, or money for college. The family may decide to celebrate with a cruise, inviting close friends and family to come along. Or la quinceañera may ask for a study trip abroad, to improve her Spanish or learn about a different culture and language.

Parents will often hold out the fifteenth birthday as a milestone, a year when more privileges will be granted—and more responsibilities expected. My mother always ticked off an entire list of privileges that would magically be conferred when my sisters and I turned fifteen. We could date boys—on double dates, that is. We could wear makeup—well, lipstick at least. We could wear high heels—sensible ones, two, three inches high at most.

In the late 1960s, when I celebrated my *quinces*, a party seemed so frivolous. Out in the world, rebellion hung in the air—the Vietnam War raged abroad and college campuses rocked with protests. César Chavez had called a national boycott of grapes in his fight to organize California's farmworkers. The Brown Berets in California and the Young Lords in New York were working in the barrios of East Los Angeles and Spanish Harlem for better housing, a greater political voice, and better education. My father proposed I go to Mexico for the summer—the summer I turned 15.

It was a perfect bridge, three months that linked the past to the present and three generations of my father's extended family to me. Great-aunts and -uncles, second and third cousins who had lived in my imagination from stories my mother had told me became real. The first half of the summer I spent in Mexico City, meeting and getting to know the branch of my grandmother's side of the family who lived there. They opened their homes to me, generously took me on trips—to the Aztec pyramids at Teotihuacán, to the mountain resort of Cuernavaca, to Tepayac to see the miraculous portrait of Our Lady of Guadalupe, the dark-skinned patron saint of the New World. There were day trips to the ancient floating gardens of Xochimilco, and to Chapultepec Park and its castle. Now a military museum, the castle was once the home of the Austrian emperor Maximilian and his wife, Carlota, where, some historians say, the empress began the quinceañera tradition as we know it today. My grandmother, who was all of six when Mexican revolution broke out, remembers her older sisters and brothers attending military balls at the castle, the girls dressing in beautiful gowns and dusting their hair with gold powder so it shimmered in the gaslight.

My fifteenth summer was filled with parties in Mexico City and in Guadalajara, where I spent the last half of my sojourn, with pampering in beauty salons, with having party dresses made or making them myself. My birthday itself passed quietly. Two cousins, the beautiful Mary Ellen, four years older than I, lithe, honey-haired, and blue-eyed, who had lived in Chicago but moved to Guadalajara ten years earlier, and Helen, six months younger than I and just as full of mischief, who was spending the summer with her grandmother, my grandmother's sister, my great-aunt Nena, in the large house at the other end of the enormous yard, took me to lunch at the Guadalajara Hilton. Three weeks later, on August 22, I wore my first evening gown to a party celebrating Nena's *santo*, her saint's day. I had stitched together the slim pink crepe empire gown, trimmed the bodice with a light green velvet ribbon, and wore it to the party with silver sling-back pumps. That night I drank my first margaritas, heard my first mariachis, was tacitly recognized by my grandmother and family, for the first time, as a young lady.

When I returned to Chicago that September, days before my junior year began, I felt different. I had discovered a confidence in myself, born of international travel. In classes in Guadalajara I had improved my French and learned to speak Spanish. I had gained pride in my culture and found a second home to which I returned no matter how unsettled my life became.

Latinos hold fast and tenderly to the quinceañera tradition for similar reasons. It highlights the very best of our cultures: the celebration of family, music, dance, attention to the most minute detail, hard work, homage to God, a wonderful feast, cooperation, and fun. At a time when our youth face tremendous challenges, we have a celebration and a tradition that honors a young girl. It is a celebration that recognizes the bright promise of her future, acknowledges her transition from a child to a woman, and lets her know that to those who care about her, she is someone very special, that she is loved. She is a fairy-tale princess for one very special day, and she will carry the memory of that day with her all her life. It will inspire her to celebrate her daughter's quince años in turn.

It is to celebrate the quinceañera—the festivities *and* the girl—that I write this book, not only to help Latinas craft celebrations but also to remind them of their own parties and themselves when they were quinceañeras. All of the chapters are based on the advice and experience of Latinas all over the country and from a variety of cultural backgrounds. For the mother or grandmother planning a quinceañera, this book offers suggestions on how to get started, how to craft a personalized religious service, and how to select a place for the party. There are suggestions for keeping track of the millions of details involved. You'll find tips for selecting dresses and invitations and for organizing your planning right up to the day of the celebration. For the girls and their families who return to their homelands, there are suggestions on how to plan celebrations there from here. And there are ideas to celebrate a fifteenth birthday without all the pomp and circumstance. There are a variety of cultural references throughout the book, but it is written so that anyone coming from any Latino culture can put together a celebration.

For the quinceañeras, I hope you find, as you turn the pages, that you are inspired to dream of the perfect way to celebrate this exciting moment in your life. For the mothers and grandmothers planning the celebration, I hope you find that the recommendations and advice offered here will help you organize the most beautiful celebration imaginable for your daughter or granddaughter, to commemorate the blossom of her youth as she flowers into a woman.

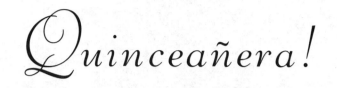

Quinceañera!

Chapter One ❦

What's the Big Deal About Turning Fifteen?

Celebrating my quince años meant beginning a life of a new adult. It has also given me much more responsibility for my own actions.

—Xochitl Comparán, Victoria, Texas

In the moments before the guests arrived at the Hialeah, Florida, banquet hall, Ileana Perez took one last look to make sure everything was perfect for her daughter's fifteenth birthday party. At the center of each table, a black velvet carousel horse with gold tack pranced, its mane and tail made of white plumes. Each of the ten places set at each of twenty tables was adorned with plastic horses filled with chocolate raisins dusted with gold. On each plate sat a white or a dark chocolate horse lollipop and a *capia*, a memento tied with a ribbon printed with the name of the guest of honor and the date. An hors d'oeuvre table filled one corner of the room. A string quartet played boleros and tangos as the guests arrived. Many of the men sported tuxedos and escorted women in sparkling sequined evening gowns and chiffon.

Perez, who immigrated from Cuba to Miami as a child, walked toward the stage, where two large pink and white flower arrangements and two waterfalls flanked a carousel. She passed the cake with a prancing horse on each of the fifteen layers, rotating on its table lit with tiny Italian lights.

FACING PAGE: *With her childhood behind her and her adulthood ahead, Patricia Correa takes a minute from her quinceañera to think of all the possibilities her future holds.* —Pilsen Photo Studio

One floor below, a white Rolls-Royce glided into the parking lot. In the back sat the guest of honor, Teresa Perez, a real-life fairy princess. A rhinestone tiara glimmered atop her long brown hair. Her dress, a white cloud of tulle, filled the back of the car. Tonight was the night she had waited for, the night her mother had planned for eighteen months. Tonight, at her quinceañera, she would be presented to her family and friends as a young woman.

In the fairy tales, the princess has to face terrible challenges before she can don the beautiful dress, go to the ball, and meet her handsome prince. There are beasts to be tamed, years of sleeping in a vine-covered tower, scrubbing and cleaning without end, and caring for dwarfs. But after going through the trial, the princess becomes a young adult.

The quinceañera is like a fairy tale in that way, too—not only for the girl but also for her parents. Together they plan the party and any religious service that may go with it. The months and sometimes years that lead up to the fiestas—the planning and financing, finding the court, practicing the dances and ordering the invitations—are part of a process that tests the honoree's maturity and her parents' patience and pocketbook. By the end, the daughter shows her parents she *can* be responsible. The parents recognize their daughter, their *niña*, is an emerging adult.

"I see her as a different person, not as a little girl that I had, but a little more grown up," said Tomás Salazar of San Antonio. He and his wife, María, threw a quinceañera for their oldest daughter Octaviana in August 1995. "I had a personal thrill walking with her down the aisle at the church. When we were introduced at the reception and we walked around the dance floor and she bowed to each corner, I felt as big as the Goodyear blimp—that's how proud I was."

This book celebrates la quinceañera, one of the most beautiful—and controversial—Latino traditions, one that is gaining in popularity in the United States. For those who want to mark the passage *de niña a mujer*, from a girl to a woman, this book can help make your fantasy quinces come true.

But why is it important to celebrate a fifteenth birthday? Why should the passage from childhood to adult be celebrated? And what does it mean, anyway?

Among the ancient cultures, the rite of passage from childhood to maturity also involved months of preparation and tests and trials. The young person had to prove he or she would be a responsible, contributing member of society. The rites of initiation emphasized religious beliefs, traditions, values, and responsibilities. They were performed when a child physically reached the adult world, when he or she became sexually mature. Those who passed the tests to prove their maturity, courage, and endurance were treated as adults and had specific responsibilities to the community. But the choices were limited. Girls' roles were often circumscribed to getting married, having children, and taking care of hearth and home. Life expectancy was less than half of what it is today. At fifteen, the average person had already lived half his or her life.

Today, biology is no longer destiny. The options for young women are almost limitless, but only one rite of passage universally commemorates their entrance into the adult world of responsibility—the driver's license. For most teens, it is the only rite of passage they go through. If they pass both parts of the test, they receive a certificate from a public institution (the state department of motor vehicles) that identifies them to the world as someone who has the skills to maneuver a vehicle on public streets, and gives them more freedom from their parents and more responsibility.

Other countries and other cultures cling to more traditional rites of passage. At thirteen, Jewish girls become "daughters of (divine) law" and assume religious responsibilities, a passage celebrated at a bas mitzvah. In Sweden, where Lutheranism is the national religion, kids go away to a religious camp for three weeks. At the end, after a confirmation ceremony, they leave as adults in the Lutheran Church, according to Michaele Haynes, curator of permanent collections at the Witte Museum in San Antonio. When the communists took over Berlin after World War II, they were able to abolish religious observance, but not the Berliners' desire for an adolescent rite of passage. The Communist Party instituted a civil rite that included a presentation and an announcement, and a pledge from the young initiate to work for the Communist state, Haynes said.

Hispanics are similarly tender and tenacious about observing their daughter's fifteenth birthday. "Where there are Hispanics, there are quinceañeras," said Maria Ramos, the owner of the Fiesta Azteca dress shop in San Antonio, Texas. San Antonio is not the only spot where quinceañeras are popular. In Phoenix, where the Hispanic population has grown 125 percent in the last decade, the quinceañera business— the dresses, shoes, crown, bouquet, favors, capias, dolls, mitts, rosaries, cushions for the gifts and for la quinceañera herself, table decorations, bands, disc jockeys, party planners, choreographers, set designers, printers, bakers, to name a few—has grown at least as much, according to Susan Orlean, in her book *Saturday Night.* "Not coincidentally, Immaculate Heart [Roman Catholic Church] was for years the site of most of Phoenix's many *quinceañeras.* . . . For a while, there were so many *quinceañeras* at Immaculate Heart that they outnumbered weddings. For that matter, there were so many *quinceañera* masses and parties that they were a standard Saturday-night social occasion in town," she wrote.

And every one is a very big deal, not only for the girl being honored, but for her parents and extended family as well, a celebration that will be rivaled only by her wedding. "It is . . . a day that the girl is going to remember for the rest of her life as a very special day," said Sister Rosa Maria Icazas of the Mexican-American Cultural Center in San Antonio. "At least for that day, she is very special to everybody. For the parents and particularly the father, it is an affirmation of their identity, and an affirmation of himself that he can give something very special to his daughter."

The quinces is not without its critics, many of whom are church officials and educators. Some say the tradition emphasizes a girl's sexuality in an age when too many teens are pregnant. Sometimes the mother, not the girl herself, wants the party. Some say the money would be better spent on a girl's education and too often after staging a quinces families are thrown into financial distress that takes months, if not years, to relieve. But Latino families, no matter how rich or how poor, time and time again make the sacrifice for a celebration that can cost as little as $2,000 or more than $100,000. "It's an expense, but it's a once-in-a-lifetime event for her," said María Salazar.

Others say it is nothing more than a way for some people to show off their wealth, whether they have it or not. Quinceañeras in Miami are legendary in extravagance and can top six figures in cost. At one such quinces held at a Miami country club, the guests were milling around the pool watching the choreographed show the court had practiced for months when they heard a helicopter. Their eyes rose to the sky as the sound of the rotors beating the air came closer until the craft appeared over the pool. The door opened and down floated la quinceañera, clinging to a tether and landing in the pool to the delight and applause of her guests. In the 1980s Miami's quinceañeras and party

planners embraced *Flashdance* as a theme. The dance sequences were so perfectly repro-
duced, including the set, that Floridians joked the only thing missing from the party
was the body double!

Church officials argue over whether the meaning of the quinceañera is lost in the
excitement of a fancy party. To guard against this, some dioceses have issued guidelines
that include a period of religious instruction, and sometimes community work. According to a Chicago priest, the ancient initiation rite on which the quinceañera is based
taught girls "to be virtuous and to care for the poor and the handicapped."

Among Mexicans, Central Americans, and Puerto Ricans, a quinceañera traditionally
begins with a Roman Catholic mass of thanksgiving. Sometimes the girl attends the regular morning mass with her parents, but most often a private mass is said in her honor
in the afternoon. The parents thank God for bringing their daughter into their lives,
and together the girl and her parents thank Him for His generosity in letting her reach
her fifteenth year. She gives her thanks for her parents and for all her good fortune.

Octaviana Salazar and her parents were very thankful they had a daughter to honor
with a party in August 1995. Two months before, Octaviana had become gravely ill
after visiting family in Laredo. "They thought it was meningitis or cholera," said her
father, Tomás Salazar. "We thought maybe we should cancel everything. But three
weeks after we brought her home, she recovered."

The quinceañera's appeal is so strong and its roots so deep that Hispanics have taken
the tradition into Protestant churches. Evangelical Lutherans, Church of Christ, Baptists, and Pentecostals are adapting the spiritual aspect of the celebration to reflect their
teachings.

While Protestant denominations are creating quinceañera services, Catholic Church
officials debate whether the celebration should be performed at all, or should be done
in such a way to discourage lavish expenditures. Because a quinceañera is not a sacrament in the Catholic Church, officials are not required to perform a mass. The archdioceses of Los Angeles and San Antonio and the diocese of Phoenix have issued
guidelines that the girls, their families, and the members of the court of honor (the
fourteen couples who attend the quinceañera and her escort) must follow before a priest
will agree to celebrate a mass. If a girl does not meet the requirements—these often

include having received the sacraments of baptism, reconciliation, and communion, being a member of the parish, and attending a specific number of conformation classes—and cannot find a priest who will say a mass anyway, many times she will forgo the ceremony and simply have the party.

The church service usually takes place the same day as the party, but not always. Mexicans and Central Americans almost always have a mass the same day. Miami's Cubans, if they have a service, will have it a week or two before the party. Celebrations among the country's suburban Latinos are less likely to include a church service.

So why do Latinos continue to celebrate quinceañeras, despite the cost, the aggravation, the criticism, and the difficulty in finding someone to perform the religious service?

Because it's a glorious celebration of family and community. Latinos love the quince años celebration as one of their most beautiful traditions. On the East Coast, they may celebrate it a year later and call it a Sweet Sixteen, but the form is the same—the ball gown, the tiara, the high-heeled shoes, the first dance with the father or the most important male figure in her life if her father isn't around, an exquisitely decorated multi-tiered cake, with bridges and fountains and dolls that represent the girl and her court. And most important, the public speech of thanks from the girl to her family—for being there when she needed them, for supporting her, for helping her sort through all a girl has to sort through today to become the best she can be.

Because it is so beautiful and because we are so proud of it, the quinceañera becomes a very positive way for non-Hispanics to learn about our culture. In Phoenix, Susan Orlean wrote, when word spread at Laura Franco-French's largely non-Hispanic private school about her quinceañera, her social stock went up considerably. "I never thought about it one way or another. But now that I'm at one of these *quinceañeras,* I'm thinking that being Hispanic might be really cool," said a classmate of Franco-French at the country club reception.

Donna Walker, a teacher in Tulsa, Oklahoma, won a state grant to teach high school students about Mexican culture by studying, planning, and organizing a quinceañera for the entire school. McLain High School is 95 percent black, and Walker saw the quinceañera project as a doorway to another culture for her students.

"They are in another world, a culture of African American society different from any other sector in town," Walker wrote on her application. "They are not living among Hispanic Americans and have limited knowledge and tolerance of the Mexican culture. This celebration of quinceañera will promote acceptance of another race and culture. Then my classroom environment becomes conducive to learning about the Mexican American."

Why reserve all this pomp and circumstance for our girls? What about our boys? Aren't they struggling with the same issues? Feeling the same pressures?

Some mothers—especially those in South Texas—have adapted the quinceañera celebration for their sons. Sister Angela Erevia, a Divine Providence nun whose book *Quince Años: Celebrando una tradición* is a key resource for Catholic priests and Protestant ministers alike, maintains the tradition should be extended to boys as well. People around McAllen, Texas, are still talking about the beau party, as quince años celebrations for boys are called, honoring Andy Closner as the social event of 1993.

Tomás Salazar of San Antonio disagrees. "I don't think it's proper for a young man. Really, twenty-one is when a young man comes out of puberty. I believe girls mature a lot faster mentally and physically. Besides, the tradition is not for boys. It's for girls."

Whether it's a fancy party, or simply going to a local dance for the first time, the Latino rite of passage often includes dancing, except where proscribed by religion. And while some Anglo priests criticize the rite as "advertising a young woman's sexual availability," a debasing view that comes from the assumption that young Hispanic women are sexually permissive, the quinceañera is a way of announcing a girl's social maturity. In some families, girls are not permitted to dance with boys other than brothers and cousins until they have had their quinceañera. In small villages in Mexico, the same rules apply at public dances until the girl dances with her father.

"In the past, la quinceañera truly was the demarcation between the age of wearing flats and high heels, between going clean-faced and wearing makeup and, at last, being allowed out to go to parties," Marilyn Goldstein, a columnist, wrote in *Newsday* in 1987.

Today, as we become more assimilated, those distinctions blur. Many young Latinas began sporting heels and lipstick years before their fifteenth birthday. In the age of baggy jeans, unisex clothes, and kids who want to be tough and hip, the quinceañera is enjoying a newfound popularity. Often when one girl among a circle of friends has a quinceañera, her friends often want a party, too. "Lisa Jomeice Teixeira's quince was the first in her Baptist church in at least ten years," Goldstein wrote. "Lisa, who lives in Island Park, said she got the idea from her friend, Maria Arroyave, who lives in Long Beach, who got the idea from her cousin. 'And if I have a daughter, I'm planning to have one for her,' Maria said. 'It's a chain reaction,' said Debbie Ganz, who discovered the tradition from her 'cousin's cousin.' "

The aggravations—the invitations that aren't ready on time, the damas or chambelanes who drop out at the last minute, the dress that isn't finished until minutes before the ceremony, and the expense—fade over time, and what are left are beautiful memories. Two years after the event, Abraham Ganz still enjoys sitting on his sofa in his Long Island home watching the video of his daughter's day yet another time—the choreographed entrance ceremony in the decorated hall, the first dance with his daughter, her first dance with her escort, the multitiered cake topped with a gazebo, the raffling off of the floral centerpieces to the guests who had the lucky tags pasted under their chairs.

Tomás and Maria Salazar threw a quince for their daughter in August 1995. Two months later, they were still paying off the bills. When a visitor asked about Octaviana's quince, they brought out the photo album, covered in pearls and white lace and pink moiré. The table decorations came from the étagère, along with the knife and server, the capias given to the guests and the corsages given to the sponsors and court. They patiently answered the visitor's questions before excusing themselves to go to the hospital, where Mrs. Salazar's son lay in the hospital struggling for life from a spray of bullets fired from an AK-47. He tried to walk away from a fight over a girl, his stepfather explained.

Despite the pain and worry, the quinceañera still casts a magic spell—sweet memories of the past and hope for the future. "You've given us a chance to remember happier times," said Tomás Salazar. "I'd recommend it to anybody and everybody. It's a real experience. The quinceañera, you won't see that birthday again, so enjoy it. Hopefully she can pass these traditions on to her own children."

❧ *Sister Angela Erevia's Top 15 Reasons* ❧ to Celebrate Quince Años

15. To deepen the faith as Christians and Catholics
14. To involve the whole family and friends in the preparations
13. To encourage young people to participate in their church and community
12. To share the responsibility and privilege of building their church
11. To evangelize the families and friends of the honoree
10. To develop spiritually by reflecting on a Christian commitment through baptism
9. To celebrate a major event in the life of the honoree
8. To celebrate with the family
7. To form or renew friendships between the generations in a family
6. To challenge ourselves and our young people to live and show our Christian values of love, forgiveness, unity, mercy, justice and peace
5. To witness together to the presence of Jesus among us
4. To share faith with the family, its young people and the entire community
3. To recognize, affirm, support, and challenge the youth
2. To join the family in thanking God for the gift of life of the youth in our community
1. To celebrate a tradition rooted in the history of our ancestors with Hispanic and indigenous origins

Chapter Two ৯

First Things First

Because this was the first quinceañera, I was lost. You have to establish who is going to do what for you and if they have a date open for you. You're talking a year ahead of time. That's why I kept everything in a book—it's so hard to remember everything.

—*Rita Aguirre, San Antonio, Texas*

Linda Alvarez had not quite turned fourteen, but planning for her quinceañera in San Antonio, Texas, was already in full swing. Her mother, Leonor, learned the hard way from throwing her older daughter's party, which she planned in six months. This time she wanted plenty of time to make sure all the details came together.

With more than a year to go, Leonor Alvarez is already looking at halls and lining up *padrinos* or sponsors, the Mexican American custom of family and close friends who contribute money or pay outright for different elements of the celebration as their gifts to the quinceañera. "They're coming to me and saying, 'I want to be the *madrina* of this or that,' " said Alvarez. Linda's uncle has already committed to buy the cake.

In Miami, Lizy Hernandez's daughter just turned thirteen. Lizy, a professional party planner, has already started thinking and saving for her daughter's celebration. "I want to have a quinces for her, but I don't want a full court of honor. She'll probably have a half court. I see a lot of girls now who are throwing big parties and having smaller

FACING PAGE: *Careful planning and good organization are the keys to a successful celebration. A notebook, preferably one with pockets, will help you keep track of all the samples, swatches, pictures, business cards and myriad other details you will acquire in the coming months.* —Richard Haro

courts, as opposed to having the traditional court of fifteen girls and fifteen guys. It depends on your budget."

So you have decided to have a quinceañera, to present your daughter to your friends in a party that could take several years to finance and at least a year to plan, and has so many details to keep under control you think your head will explode!

You are about to do nothing less than craft a bash that reflects your taste as well as your daughter's, must appeal to at least two and sometimes as many as four generations of your family, and at the same time echoes your daughter's dreams and fantasies. The time you spend together creating this event will be invaluable for both of you, strengthening your relationship and bringing you closer. The quinceañera will learn from you how to make her dreams come true, a process that often requires hard work and careful planning. And you in turn will learn that your daughter is no longer a little child, but a young woman with ideas of her own, ready to accept more responsibility for herself as she moves toward adulthood. The traditions of your culture, your family, and your community all help determine how you start organizing the celebration and what elements you will include.

The Elements of a Quinceañera

The elements included in a quince años celebration vary from culture to culture, and even from region to region within the United States. The Spanish word for the celebration itself varies: Latinos from the Caribbean use the masculine form, *quinceañero,* while most other cultures refer both to the honoree and the party itself as the feminine, *quinceañera.* Whatever you call your celebration, it should include those elements that mean the most to you and best reflect who you are.

- **The honor escort.** Whether he is called *un chambelán* (among Mexicans), *escorte* (among Puerto Ricans), or *galán* (Dominican), he is always *de honor* (of honor). The honor escort accompanies the quinceañera throughout the festivities. He can be a brother, a cousin, a friend, an uncle, or even her father.

- **The court of honor.** Traditionally fourteen girls and fourteen boys, each couple representing a year of her life, who stand with the quinceañera on her special day. But the quinceañera may choose to have just seven couples, each person representing a year, or a unisex court of all boys or all girls, or even just one *dama de honor* (maid of honor). They are her supporting cast, the friends and family who are nearest to her in age and dearest to her in her heart. In addition, the court may include flower girls, who sprinkle petals on the ground so the quinceañera walks on a fragrant path. Central American families often include a prince and princess, tiny children dressed identically to the quinceañera and the honor escort, as symbols of innocence.

- **Padrinos, or sponsors.** A Mexican American custom that ideally spreads the economic burden of the party among the extended family and close family friends. Each sponsor either contributes cash or buys a specific element of the celebration, such as the cake, the napkins, or the drinks, as a gift to the quinceañera.

- **A religious celebration.** A mass, a church service, or even a simple blessing. Generally, Cuban families forgo a church service. Mexicans, Mexican Americans, and Central Americans nearly always have one. Church services for Puerto Rican quinceañeras traditionally include the blessing of all the accessories used during the reception. At that time, her mother places a tiara on the quinceañera's head and her father changes her shoes from flats to heels.

- **A reception,** which may be organized around a specific theme, such as carousel horses, a French garden, a popular movie, or a television soap opera. The reception includes:

  The introduction of the court of honor. The master of ceremonies announces the names of each person in the court, sometimes with very brief description of their relationship to the quinceañera.

  The presentation of the quinceañera. This is the big moment, when the quinceañera enters the room. Cuban girls often make very elaborate entrances on a spotlit stage with a set built just for the occasion. Her father will escort her to the edge of the dance floor, where she curtsies to her guests. Puerto Rican girls walk in on the arm of their escort to a white peacock chair decorated with ribbons, where she sits while the tiara is placed on her head and her shoes are changed from flats to heels.

The choreography or *vals* (waltz). Among Cuban Americans, the choreography generally begins before the presentation with one or two dances performed by the court of honor. The choreography resumes with the quinceañera dancing with her father, then with her honor escort. The court of honor joins them on the dance floor in a series of choreographed numbers. Other cultures generally begin with the quinceañera dancing with her father, usually to a waltz. She continues to dance with her father for the second number and her escort dances with her mother. Halfway through that song they switch, so the quinceañera is dancing with her escort and her parents are dancing with each other. For the third number, the rest of the court joins in. Special dances may be included in the choreography for the grandfather or uncles or other important family members to have a solo dance with the quinceañera.

The *brindis*, or toast. Sometimes led by the father, but usually by the master or mistress of ceremonies.

The thank-you. The parents may want to read a thank-you to the girl for turning out so well and to God for bringing her to the day of her celebration. The girl also reads a thank-you, including her parents for being there as well as for the party, and her guests for coming.

- **The dinner.** This can be an elaborate, catered sit-down affair or a buffet made by a member of the family assisted by an army of helpers.
- **The dance.** A band, a disc jockey, or both may provide the music to get people out of their chairs and partying hardy.

The Notebook of Dreams

A year and a half before her daughter's party, Ileana Perez of Miami began gathering her thoughts and talking with her daughter, Teresa, about how they wanted Teresa's quinceañera to be. They started with the theme—carousel horses. Ileana Perez owned a carousel horse, which she wanted to use as one of the decorations at the party. And she

Elena Romero of New York City sits in the peacock chair bedecked with ribbons and lace, where moments before the pearl crown was placed on her head and her shoes were changed from flats to heels, part of her presentation to society. —Courtesy of the Romero family

knew she wanted to hold the party in a room with a stage from which Teresita could make an impressive entrance—her presentation.

"I started doing a lot of thinking and planning," said Ileana Perez. "I have a portfolio like this full of things. Every time I thought of something I would write it down."

The details of putting together such a grand party will soon become a mass of confusion unless they are saved in one place from the beginning. Organization is the key, and what better place to put all those little details than a binder or notebook, preferably one with pockets as well as paper.

Ileana Perez kept meticulous notes concerning what she wanted and what she found—flower arrangements, menus, banquet halls, fabrics, dress designers and seamstresses, disc jockeys, limousine services, printers, invitation styles—anything and everything she thought she might need or want or saw, where each item could be found and how much it would cost. "It's like Christmas shopping you do a year and a half before," said Perez.

Your own notebook of dreams can be as fancy as a Filofax or a simple college notebook. Label each section with a major expense: church, hall, music, catering, the cake, the decorations, and so on. Pockets are useful to keep brochures, fabric swatches, prices, and eventually, receipts for deposits and payments you make. All the details are in one place so that they can come to life on a very special day.

WHAT TO INCLUDE IN YOUR NOTEBOOK OF DREAMS

- If you are planning to have a religious service, each church you plan to contact, its address and telephone number, the name of the contact person. The requirements they have: what sacraments the quinceañera and often her parents must have received, whether classes or a retreat are required, the price, any decorating restrictions, the dates they have available, whether you must belong to the parish or congregation, whether you can adapt the service to include special readings or music you may want.
- Information about reception sites: The size of the room, the dance floor or stage, whether they have any special decorations for a quinceañera, such as a pumpkin

coach, a peacock chair, a clamshell, or an archway for the presentation or entrance of the quinceañera and her court. Note the layout of the room, what kind of loud-speaker system and lights are available, the color of the room.

- Each party professional you would like to work with should have a separate section: party planners, choreographers, photographers, caterers, dressmakers or bridal shops, florists, printers, videographers, hair stylists, limousines. Include names, phone numbers, and prices and details of packages being offered.

- The court of honor: their names, addresses, and phone numbers.

- The guest list: the names and addresses of the people you plan to invite.

- Ideas for dresses for the quinceañera and her court: pictures of dresses, fabric swatches, headpieces for the girls; pictures of tuxedos or other attire, formal-wear shops for the boys; prices for everything.

- Music selections you would like played at the church service and for the presentation, the waltz, and the dance.

- Musicians, disc jockeys, and mariachis for the church, the reception, the cocktail hour, the dance—wherever you want music played.

- Ideas for themes, colors, decorations, and favors. If you decide to make them yourself, jot down the materials you will need, where they are available, and how much they will cost.

- Your budget: how much you have to spend and how you want to spend it.

- The padrinos and madrinas, if you are including them. Whom you plan to ask, whom you have asked, how they responded, what they will sponsor; if they give cash, the amount they gave. If they are buying an element outright, ask them for copies of the receipts.

- A list of newspapers that run quinceañera announcements on the social pages, including their addresses, telephone numbers, copy requirements, and deadlines.

- A twelve-month calendar.

- A ruler and/or tape measure.

Setting the Date and Choosing the Colors

Tradition throughout the Latino world calls for the quinceañera to be held on the day of the girl's fifteenth birthday, but it's usually held on the Saturday closest to her birthday. When quinceañera celebrations were held at home, the families had more control over when they threw the party. But now that quinceañeras are more frequently hosted in rented halls and hotel ballrooms, you may not always get the date you want. It pays to pick several dates. Try to avoid the anniversary of the death of a family member.

If you are having a church service, call the church office first not only to see what they require of you and your family but also to see if the dates are available. The same

❧ ❧ Birthstones and Flowers ❧ ❧

MONTH	BIRTHSTONE	COLOR	FLOWER
January	garnet	dark red	snowdrop or carnation
February	amethyst	purple	primrose or violet
March	aquamarine or bloodstone	light blue-green or green with red	violet or jonquil
April	diamond	white	daisy or sweetpea
May	emerald	green	hawthorn or lily of the valley
June	pearl, alexandrite, or moonstone	pearl, green and red	rose
July	ruby	red	water lily or larkspur
August	sardonyx or peridot	red or yellow-green	poppy or gladiolus
September	sapphire	blue	morning glory or aster
October	opal or tourmaline	opalescent or multicolor	hops or calendula
November	topaz	yellow, red, or pink	chrysanthemum
December	turquoise or lapis lazuli	blue	holly or narcissus

❦ ❦ *Coming of Age Among the Quechua* ❦ ❦

The coming of age among the Quechua, an indigenous people of the Andes, requires as much preparation of those being honored as their parents. The ceremonies are always celebrated at the beginning of February, in conjunction with Candlemas, according to Ramiro Matos, a visiting curator at the Smithsonian Institution's Museum of the American Indian. There are similar ceremonies for boys as well as girls, signifying their transition to adulthood. As such, they have adult responsibilities, have reached sexual maturity, and are available for marriage.

The young people have to go through a period of preparation to qualify for the rite at Candlemas, Matos said. "They have to do public work, such as cleaning the streets and tending livestock and fields. They support the celebration in honor of the Virgin, they take care of the horse used by the priest, and they wash the church floor. They agree to perform public works for a month or two."

Chicha, a kind of beer, is made especially for the initiation ceremony. In the girl's rite, "the baptismal godmother has the obligation to counsel her. After these rites, since they are celebrated during Candlemas, they dance and party. There's a lot of food," said Matos.

It is at these celebrations that a love interest often begins and leads to marriage. "This indigenous quinceañera is a preparation for marriage. The young man and young woman are socially qualified and morally qualified for marriage," said Matos.

goes for a reception site. If you plan to have the church service and the reception on the same day and you find places that are available on the date you want, secure them as soon as possible with deposits. Most churches and reception sites will not hold a date unless they have the required deposit and a signed contract.

Early in the planning, you might also pick the color scheme. Traditionally, you pick the color of your birth gem. If you do not like it, then throw tradition out the window and pick whatever color you want.

Choosing a Theme

Among Cuban Americans, the theme for the celebration is one of the most important decisions to be made. It can be anything from a flower, such as roses or lilies, a recent movie release, or an interest, such as art or a French garden. Whatever the quinceañera's fantasy is, however she would like to enter the adult world, that can be her theme. It is echoed in the table decorations and the invitations, and is interpreted in the choreography. Popular themes include fairy tales, such as Cinderella, Sleeping Beauty, and the Little Mermaid; themes from movies or TV shows like *Flashdance* or *Star Trek;* a time period, such as Victorian, with lots of lace and ribbons, tiny roses and parasols, or the Renaissance or the Middle Ages, complete with damsels, knights, and castles; a favorite toy or hobby, such as horses, teddy bears, angels, or Barbie.

A choreographer or party planner can be of tremendous help in choosing and executing a theme. Esthersita Penton Nodarse, one of the first party planners in Miami to coordinate quinceañera celebrations, planned and choreographed a celebration for a girl who had studied ballet for a number of years. The girl chose Dream . . . Star . . . Fantasy as her theme. She made her entrance sitting on a shimmering gold star that was lowered from the ceiling. She performed a ballet solo, and after waltzing with her father, she danced with the six boys in her court of honor.

Rosendo Ramon, a Miami choreographer, had one quinceañera who was a fashion model and wanted to use the modeling theme for her celebration. For her presentation, she stood in a large picture frame, and struck several poses, finally walking through the frame to the applause of her adoring family and friends.

Themes are as limitless as your imagination.

Setting a Budget: How Much Will This Cost, Anyway?

A quinceañera can be a simple buffet dinner and party at home with a disc jockey or an elaborate ball at the Ritz Carleton Hotel in Palm Beach, with a choreographed presentation, a sit-down dinner for 200, and dancing to a live band through the wee hours of the morning. The more details you plan to include, the larger the price tag. Some celebrations in Miami, with specially designed lights and sets for the presentation, fresh roses flown in to perfectly match the color of the court of honor's dresses, three different musical groups to play for the cocktail hour, and the dinner and the dance, all celebrated in a hotel ballroom, have topped $100,000. Others in New York's Washington Heights section of Manhattan were great successes at less than $1,000, held at home, with a homemade buffet, a disc jockey, a simple street dress rather than a ball gown, and no court of honor. It all depends on the quinceañera and her family.

It's important to know what you want and how you want to spend your money. Once you have established your priorities, you will know in which areas you will want to spend more money and where you will want to cut corners. These are some questions to ask yourself before you establish a firm budget.

- Do we want a traditional, formal celebration, or one that is smaller and more informal?
- How large will your court of honor be? Will you invite the family of each participant? Or are just the parents invited to the reception?
- How many people will you invite?
- Where do you want to hold your celebration? At home? At a country club? At a banquet hall? In the church hall? Or at another place that will give you the kind of setting you want?
- Will you want live music throughout the celebration, with a string quartet playing during the cocktail hour and dinner and a band for the dance? Or do you prefer a disc jockey to play through the night?

- What kind of dinner do you want? A formal sit-down dinner with waiters serving each course? A family-style banquet, where the waiters bring large platters of food to the table and everyone serves himself or herself? A buffet, either catered or prepared in the homes of family and friends?
- Do you want entertainment during dinner—a folkloric dance group, for example, or folk musicians that reflect your culture?
- If you are having a church service, what is included in the price? Music? Decorations?
- What kind of decorations do you want at the reception? What kind of favors will you give your guests?

As you begin to shop for each element of the celebration, you will quickly get an idea of how much the whole thing will cost and how much each of your suppliers will want you to put down as a deposit to secure their services on a particular date. If you don't get prices to enable you to know how much things will cost, your budget will not be realistic. Remember to leave a 20 percent cushion for unexpected expenses such as sponsors who are unable to come through at the last minute or a tuxedo rental for the replacement for a member of the court who drops out.

When it comes to quinceañeras, time is often more valuable than money. With enough time, you can buy what you need as you go along and save the money for the deposits. Even with a budget it's not always easy to estimate how much everything will cost. Little unanticipated expenses crop up here and there, and the celebration nearly always ends up costing more than you think.

Most people start saving money for the celebration as soon as they think about having one. Julie Martinez of Chicago was only ten years old when her family started saving money for her quinceañera. "My dad had a big black box from work, and each one of us, we put something in there," said her younger sister, Marisela. "When my sister decided she wanted a quinceañera, each day we started putting in more and more money, and that's how we raised it all. My sister had her party in Mexico, so the family there helped, too." When Julie's party was over, the Martinezes started saving for Marisela's celebration, which they held three years later in Chicago.

Every week for a year and a half before their daughter's party, Tomás and María Salazar of San Antonio salted away $30. Sponsors covered many of the expenses, but not everyone who agreed to be a sponsor was able to honor their commitment when the time came. Months later, the Salazars were still paying off expenses from the $5,500 party that brought together four hundred friends and relatives from as far away as Nuevo Laredo and Delaware.

In most Latino cultures, the girl's parents pay for most, if not all, of the expenses, although extended family members may help make decorations or food, or find a band or hall, or lend a hand with anything else that might be needed. It's part of their gift to the quinceañera. Ileana Perez of Miami said that her family got together on a regular basis to make the decorations for her daughter's quinceañero in December 1995. The gathering of the extended family, especially the women, to prepare and share ideas for the celebration not only spreads out some of the preparation tasks but also strengthens and renews family ties.

The celebration brings the family together not just for the party but for the entire year of preparation. In San Antonio, the Leal family divided the tasks, so everyone was in charge of something. Diana Leal Sandoval, the oldest daughter, made the decorations, while her mother coordinated the church, the club, and the band. Sisters, cousins, and aunts worked throughout the year on the centerpieces.

In other instances, for example, a godmother may volunteer to take care of the capias, the printed ribbon favors given to guests to commemorate the celebration, or an aunt will buy or make the table decorations or a cousin will buy all the *cerámicas*—

Quinceañera or Sweet Sixteen?

The tradition may be to debut at fifteen among Latinos, but the North American influence is having an effect. In the Northeast, many Latinas put their quinceañera off a year and call it a Sweet Sixteen. Never mind that all the trappings are the same—the ball gown, the escorts, the court of honor, the choreography, the changing of the shoes, and for some, the church service of thanksgiving. "I think it all depends on when the family has the money," said the Reverend Juana Villavicencio, the pastor of the United Church of Christ in Danbury, Connecticut.

ceramic favors given to the guests at Central American and Caribbean American celebrations. It is a way of telling the quinceañera that she is very special to those people,
that they are there for her in celebration, and that they will remain with her on her journey to womanhood.

PADRINOS—YOUR SPONSORING ANGELS

In most cultures, help from the extended family and friends is informal, but Mexican
Americans have a formal tradition and role for those who help. They are the padrinos—the sponsors or godparents, who contribute toward what sometimes seems like
every detail of the celebration, from the girl's dress to the ice for the drinks. The sponsors are members of the extended family or close family friends who agree to help with
the expenses either by giving money or by selecting and paying for an element of the
celebration outright. Their contributions are formally acknowledged in the invitations
and the programs, with lists of sponsors sometimes numbering more than a hundred.
The most important sponsors—those who give the five traditional gifts of the crown,
the medal, the earrings, the bracelet, and the rosary and Bible—are often part of the
procession into the church service and the reception.

Many families begin their planning by lining up their sponsors. Some will volunteer
to give specific items. Others will give a cash contribution to the party. The money you
gather from sponsors plus your own savings for the celebration are a good nest egg from
which you can pay any deposits or other cash outlays.

Bear in mind, however, that sometimes a sponsor who promised to pay for the band
or contribute money for the videographer may have a change of fortune and be unable to
come through. If that happens, you will be happy to have your 20 percent reserve in your
budget that was mentioned earlier. All you can do is try to plan for just such emergencies
and work around them when they happen so your celebration can go on as planned.

PACKAGES AND MORE PACKAGES

As you shop around, you will find just about everyone offers packages: formalwear and bridal shops, catering and banquet halls. With all the prices you have gathered in your notebook, you will be able to determine whether the package is a good deal or whether you would do better buying each thing separately on your own. You can use this information to negotiate a lower price.

What packages offer are convenience. At the dressmaker, you may be able to get not only the dresses for the quinceañera and the girls in her court of honor but also invitations, a photographer, a videographer, table decorations and favors for the guests—even a limousine. The owner of a restaurant or banquet hall may offer packages that include food and beverages, the orchestra or disc jockey, and room decorations.

Remember, everything should be negotiable, from the price of the package to what it includes. If a limousine is included in a package, and your brother-in-law, who owns a limo company, is giving your daughter a limo to ride in on her special day, ask to have it left out and the total price reduced. Just asking for a

Tips for Hiring a Party Planner

♦ Check out your consultant with your friends and the other professionals you have started to meet through your own planning efforts. Ask for references and check with the local chamber of commerce or Better Business Bureau to see if any complaints have been filed. Most clients and coordinators find each other by word of mouth.

♦ A deposit is generally required up front, to give the planner some cash to pay for deposits or for items that you approve. But the deposit should only be a percentage of the entire cost of the party. "If you pay someone off at the beginning, they may slack off," said Hernandez.

♦ Meet with several coordinators. You have to feel comfortable with the person who is planning your quinces. After all, he or she becomes a part of your life for a year or so.

♦ When you meet with the consultant, ask which professional organizations or local business groups he or she belongs to. Find out what his or her background, experience, and qualifications are. What is the largest or smallest quinces he or she has coordinated? What parts of the celebration will he or she be able to oversee—the church, the reception, the choreography?

♦ Once you agree on the services the coordinator will provide, get a contract specifying what you have agreed to. The contract should include due dates for your payments and the coordinator's delivery of services.

discount can save you between 5 and 15 percent of the total cost. On a $5,000 party, that can put $250 to $750 back in your pocket.

Party Planners and Consultants

If the demands on your time are great, consider hiring someone to do the legwork for you. Most Latino party planners and wedding consultants organize quinceañeras as well. For 10 to 15 percent of the total price of the party, they will help you avoid mistakes and ultimately save you not only time but money as well. Party coordinators can offer several levels of service, from orchestrating the entire party so that all you have to do is pick the date to providing a package of services to giving you an idea of what you will need and where to find it within your budget. Some also offer several payment options, either a deposit and one or two additional payments or a fixed sum every month.

Lizy Hernandez, a party coordinator in South Florida, sits down with the quinceañera and her mother nine months to a year before the party to talk about what they have in mind. "Everything else is up to me. I know what they can and can't afford. The mother has no running around to do. I do it all for her, and I just call her and say, 'Listen, this is within your budget. When can we meet?' I will set appointments for the mother and daughter, around their schedules. I do all the legwork for them."

Like most party planners, Hernandez has a core of suppliers she works with regularly to provide the elements of the party. And that can work in the quinceañera's favor, because she can get discounts—sometimes as much as 20 to 30 percent—that others off the street cannot get. "I have particular people I work with, who I know will do me proud," said Lizy. "Because it's my name, it's my reputation, so I surround myself with only the best."

Susana Martinez did not use a party planner for her daughter Marisela's celebration in Chicago, but she relied heavily on the advice of the dressmaker she used for everything from the clothing to the choreography. The dressmaker found the shoes for the court of honor and arranged to have them dyed, so the girls not only had the same style but the same color as well. When Martinez could not find a formal-wear shop that had a white tuxedo small enough to fit her youngest son, the dressmaker found a tuxedo for her.

Whose Party Is It, Anyway?

The quinceañera is so special, and there are so many decisions to make. Sometimes each of the two principal planners—the quinceañera and her mother—has very strong ideas of what she wants. Sometimes they agree, but many times they do not. The potential for conflict is built in, as mother and daughter must negotiate compromise after compromise so the celebration can take place.

Father Francisco Macías's office lies in the shadow of San Antonio's San Fernando Cathedral. Inside a mother and daughter wait to talk with him about a quinceañera mass in the 240-year-old church. He opens their meeting with a question for each of them:

"Who is going to be the quinceañera? You? Or you? If you and your daughter decide to have the quinceañera together, you have to do it peacefully," Macías said.

The most successful quinceañeras are the ones that daughter and mother produce together, with suggestions from the extended family as well. The quinceañera basks in the spotlight, but understands that her family shines that day as well.

As a child, Ileana Perez had dreamed of having her own quinceañera in her native Cuba. But the revolution that put Fidel Castro and the Communists in power replaced her fantasy with the reality of fleeing her island homeland with her family and settling in Miami.

"I couldn't have a party for my own fifteenth birthday," Perez recalled, as she attended to last-minute details for her daughter, Teresa's, debut. "Everything ended when we came here. I said that my daughter would have a party like this. She's been part of every single detail in this place."

Teresa Perez wanted and went on a cruise for her fifteenth birthday. Her grandmother insisted she have a party as well, and Teresa, known as Teresita, recognized how important it was to her grandmother and her mother. "My mom never had a fifteen, so this is like my mom's fifteen and the cruise was like my fifteen," Teresita Perez said.

During the planning stages the quinceañera often feels she must prove to her family that she is not a baby anymore, trying to get her parents to recognize she has become a young woman in deed as well as in appearance. "Maturity involves being honest and true to oneself, making decisions based on a conscious internal process, assuming responsibility for one's decisions, having healthy relationships with others, and developing one's own true gifts," writes Mary Pipher in her best-selling book *Reviving Ophelia: Saving the Lives of Adolescent Girls.*

That does not mean that the process is easy, or that you and your mother will not disagree. But you will learn important skills in the planning process—organizing a big event, compromising with people, sharing, and learning to have patience. With six months to go before her celebration, Maria Magaña of Cicero, a Chicago suburb, and her mother, Leticia Magaña, argued over everything from who would stand in the court of honor to the color of Maria's dress. "Maria keeps saying that it's *her* quince años. I tell her yes, but that does not mean we're going to do whatever she wants," said Leticia Magaña.

According to Father Macías, most often the girls object not so much to their parents setting limits, but to the way in which the limits are set. Too often the mothers try their best to give their daughters the celebration *they* never had, the one the mother always wanted, regardless of her daughter's wishes and taste. When the mother and daughter unconsciously compete to be la quinceañera and the mother pulls rank to have things done her way, it can be hurtful to their relationship, Macías said. He often has to point this out to agitated mothers.

When tensions arise between young girls and their mothers, these tips will help restore calm.

TIPS FOR MOMS

- Take time to think about why giving your daughter a quinceañera celebration is important to you. Be honest with yourself. Are you making the quinceañera you wanted for yourself? Or a celebration that you want to give her and she wants to have?
- Sit down with your daughter early on and talk about ideas you want to include.

❧ ❧ De Niña a Mujer ❧ ❧

Your quinceañera may be around the corner, but your parents still look at you as more of a child than a young woman. Taking an active role in planning your celebration is a way to show your parents that you are growing up, that you can act responsibly.

• Ask your mother what tasks need to be done for the celebration and take on several tasks for yourself.

• Find the names and phone numbers of dressmakers, catering halls, people to make the decorations, bakers to make the cake, choreographers, disc jockeys, bands, or whatever other professionals are needed. Find out how much they cost and whether they are available on the day you want.

• Encourage your mother to use you as a sounding board for the decisions about your party she is wrestling with and do the same with her.

• Offer suggestions you think you both can live with.

In other words, show your parents you *are* responsible by acting responsibly.

What aspects of the celebration are important to you? Which don't you care so much about? Find out which are important to her. From there you can decide on what you can do her way, where you will both have to compromise, and where you will have to stand firm.

• Ask for your daughter's help in finding the banquet hall, choosing the decorations, selecting the invitations, and doing whatever else needs to be done. The tradition of the celebration lies not only in the party itself, but in the planning and preparation. The skills you teach her to organize such a grand celebration she will use again to help you when you have a quinces for her younger sister, and for her daughter as well.

• Set clear and firm limits when necessary, but let your daughter make decisions and choices within those limits.

• Remember that perfection is attained only in heaven.

TIPS FOR DAUGHTERS

- Think about what aspects of the quinceañera are important to you.
- Sit down with your mother and tell her how you feel about those aspects and why. See which ones she agrees with and which she does not, as well as her reasons.
- Latino cultures respect and encourage the mother-daughter bond, while Anglo culture often encourage teenage girls to separate from their mothers. Figure out what *you* think so you can distinguish between pressures from the outside and what you believe and want.
- Take time to develop your own ideas about the party, instead of simply reacting to what your mother or other members of the family want. Which are the same? Which are different?
- If you want your mother to acknowledge and respect your choices about your celebration, know why you want what you want and be able to explain your reasons to her. Do not forget to separate what you think from what you feel—they are not the same!

Taking an active role in planning and producing their celebrations gives girls a sense of accomplishment, pride, and self-esteem. By incorporating their own interests—whether it's dance, art, modeling, music, athletics, science, or singing—into the celebration, they share a part of themselves with their guests. The effort that went into exploring those interests is validated and rewarded.

Planning a quinceañera celebration is a tremendous opportunity to bring mother and daughter closer, to improve communication, boost appreciation for each other's skills and talents, and engender mutual respect. Laura Valenzuela of Chicago took an active interest in her party planning from the beginning. When she and her mother made the decision to have a quinceañera, Laura started calling banquet halls to gather prices and details. Together she and her mother, Ana Maria, narrowed the prospects down to five. Together they visited each one, and together they made a decision about which one to rent.

AND WHAT ABOUT PAPI?

Traditionally, the father finances the celebration, but the realization of it sits squarely on mother's shoulders. When fathers are actively involved in the planning and preparation, the family becomes closer, communication among everyone improves, and everyone in the immediate family is pleased with the celebration.

When the Nietos of Chicago decided to have a quinceañera for their daughter, Michele, Rolando Nieto wanted to be as involved in the preparations as his wife, Esther. Together they looked for fabric, consulted with the seamstress, picked out favors. "They were things that concerned both of us," said Nieto. "We talked about everything."

The Nietos believed that nothing should be done unless they and Michele agreed. They discussed every detail, every decision that had to be made. Nothing was dictated. The result was a party that made everyone happy and was tailor-made for Michele, beginning with the church service.

Chapter Three &

God Is Traveling with You:
Your Spirituality and the Religious Ceremony

> With a church service, it's like I'm actually being accepted as a woman, not only socially, but by God. It's pretty neat.
>
> —*Dominique Estell Chavez, San Antonio, Texas*

Organizing the party consumes much of the effort and generates much of the excitement of a quinceañera celebration, but among some Latin cultures, a religious service is the most important element of coming of age. No matter how simple, the church ceremony acknowledges that your spiritual side, too, is growing. It is a time to give thanks for our lives, our blessings, and our families, whether they are present with us in the church or merely in our hearts.

Religion has always had a part in coming-of-age celebrations, going back to ancient stone temples of Mexico, said Manuel Vasquez, who is Cuban and a religion historian at the University of Florida at Gainesville. "It resonates with some elements of Pentecostal churches," said Vasquez. "It is very emotive and spectacular." The Spaniards christianized the ceremony, along with the population, and brought the tradition to Puerto Rico and Cuba.

But over the years, the religious component of the coming of age celebration has

FACING PAGE: *A young girl presents flowers to the Virgin Mary during her mass at a church in Guadalupe, Arizona.* —Chicano Research Collection, Department of Archives and Manuscripts, University Libraries, Arizona State University, Tempe.

been eclipsed by the effort and expense many families put into the more secular element of the celebration: the party. As more Latinos move to Protestant churches, the Catholic Church is trying to reclaim those traditions, which have become secularized in the United States, what Vasquez calls "a fast-food type of ritual."

While some Hispanics criticize the Catholic Church for trying to dampen their enthusiasm for the quinceañera, historians credit the Church with saving the tradition in Puerto Rico after the United States invasion in 1898. "The Catholic Church became more influential after 1898 because it was one of the institutions that remained intact after the U.S. invasions," said José López, a Puerto Rican historian in Chicago. Because Puerto Rico's upper classes were more closely aligned with the Church, the quinceañera celebrations among Puerto Rico's wealthy were more likely to have a religious element.

Most of the time, the church service takes place on the same day as the party. In Miami, however, the custom among Mexicans, Colombians, and Central Americans is to hold the service a week earlier. The quinceañera and her family and the court and their families get together for a brunch after the church service.

Because most Latinos are Catholic, we most often seek a mass to celebrate our quince años. While young Latinas may attend church with their families, the quinceañera is one of the few times teens seek out the church on their own. They want to be there, and Father Arturo Perez, an expert on popular Latino expressions of faith, believes it is a chance for the church to welcome them. "It is an opportunity to touch the lives of young people, not just from a religious point of view, but also an opportunity to say the church can be for them. We've always included the sacrament of reconciliation in our preparation, but we talk about it on their level, what it's really meant to be. It's not meant to put them down, but to give them a place to vent and to come in contact with a God, who basically wants to be with them."

The quinceañera is not a sacrament in any church, but a popular cultural expression of our faith in God. Since the church does not require a girl to have a quinceañera, the celebration in some dioceses and parishes is controversial. Concerned that people spend too much time, money, and attention on the trappings, Catholic archdioceses in Los Angeles and San Antonio and the diocese of Phoenix have issued guidelines for prospective quinceañeras and their families to follow. Private masses are discouraged in favor of group celebrations, an arrangement that has brought some degree of resentment in the Hispanic communities where they have been issued.

In other cities, such as New York and Chicago, the decision to offer quinceañera masses and the religious preparation required are left to the individual parishes. Some priests will do them, while others will not. Some require three months of conformation classes; others, none. The result is that people "shop around" for a church where they feel they can have the celebration they want.

As more Latinos convert to Protestant churches, we are bringing the quinceañera tradition with us. Lutheran, Methodist, Baptist, Pentecostal, and even nondenominational churches have developed services thanking God for bringing the quinceañera to her fifteenth birthday and asking for divine guidance and protection through the rest of her life. The Reverend Susan Birkelo, pastor of Iglesia Luterana La Trinidad in Chicago, regards the quinceañera service as "an affirmation of baptism; another opportunity to affirm young people, to help them live out what they believe." Although the quinceañera is not part of the Lutheran tradition, Latino Lutherans are asking for the ceremony—so much so that the Evangelical Lutheran Church in America has included a liturgy for the celebration of a fifteenth birthday in their new worship books, to give Anglo pastors an idea of what the celebration is and how the service of thanksgiving should run.

At La Rabaña Church in Chicago, an independent Bible congregation, a special committee of church members helps the family plan and prepare for the religious service of thanksgiving as well as the reception afterward. "When the parents go out of their way in making such a big event for them, it brings the girl more to the seriousness of life," said the Reverend Ruth Mercado, co-pastor of La Rabaña. "She thinks of the future and wants to meet her parents' standards. She'll want to be something after that."

The church celebration stirs our emotions. As our parents see us on the threshold of adulthood, they remember us as the tiny children we were just a few short years ago. And it is emotional for us, too, as we think of their love for us, of our sorrow to leave childhood behind, and of our excitement to be on the brink of a new stage in our lives.

What Makes a Service

The quinceañera services vary from denomination to denomination, and sometimes even from parish to parish or congregation to congregation. Often the service will include these elements:

- A greeting or prayer offered by the priest or minister to welcome everyone to the ceremony and to ask God's blessing.
- Scripture readings from the Old and New Testaments are selected based on the denomination, the structure of the service, and what the quinceañera and the pastor want to express about this important moment in the girl's life.
- Baptismal vows or promises are often renewed as part of the ceremony, either by the quinceañera by herself or with the members of the court. Sometimes the girl's baptismal candle is brought to the church and relit either by her alone or by her with her baptismal godparents.
- A prayer or dedication or thanksgiving is said by the girl, offering her more mature life to God's service and thanking him for her first fifteen years of life with all its blessings.
- Presentation of fifteen red roses is made to the girl herself during a Protestant service or to the altar of the Virgin Mary in a Catholic service. Each rose represents a year of the girl's life and stands for her blossoming into a woman. A family member—a grandmother or aunt—may present the roses to the girl. In a Catholic ceremony the girl then places them on the altar of the Virgin Mary. In a Mexican Catholic service where sponsors are used, the person who bought the roses gives them to the girl and together they place them on the altar of the Virgin Mary.
- The blessing and presentation of gifts to the quinceañera. Five traditional gifts are made to the girl from her family or sponsors:

    The prayer book and rosary or Bible keep the word of God in her life.

    The crown designates her as a queen before God.

The medal or cross and necklace proclaims her Christianity.
The bracelet or ring represents the unending circle of God's love.
The earrings remind her to hear God's word.

Questions for the Pastor

Different churches have different requirements for the quinceañera service. You might want to ask the pastor:

* Whether the family must be parish members or members at a parish that does not perform quinceañeras. Registration may take several months. The church office has to verify the records of the quinceañera's sacraments.
* Whether private services are offered, or only group services.
* What religious requirements there are. Must the girl have completed certain sacraments? Must she be enrolled in religious education classes?
* If there are restrictions or requirements for the court of honor.
* Who decorates the church?

ẟ ẟ Blessings in Puerto Rico ẟ ẟ

The five traditional gifts are sometimes all a minister will allow to be blessed during the church service, but among Puerto Ricans who preserve the customs of the island, many items are brought to the church for the priest's blessing. The quinceañera's shoes, which are changed during the service from the flats in which she enters the church to the heels her parents place on her feet during the mass; the decorated glasses used to toast her at the reception; the photo album that will hold her memories of her special day; the doll decorated with the capias that she will give to her guests—everything that is made for her celebration is brought to the church and blessed so that her first day in her new stage of life is permeated with God's grace.

§ § *A Quinceañera Celebrated Before the World* § §

The archdiocese of San Antonio, Texas, tries to encourage group quinceañera masses whenever possible, as a way of reducing the demand on priests to perform these celebrations and cutting down on the pomp, expense, and extravaganza. So for the girls who have just signed up for religious education classes in any parish in San Antonio, the diocese gives them an incentive: If they stay in the classes for an entire year, they can participate in the group quinceañera mass at San Fernando Cathedral on the first Sunday in May. The celebration takes place at the nine o'clock service and is broadcast throughout the Spanish-speaking world via satellite. The church picks up the expenses for the dresses and holds a very simple reception after the mass for the girls, their families, and anyone else who wants to attend.

- Whether videographers and photographers are allowed to shoot during the service. Does the family hire its own videographer or must they hire the one recommended by the church?
- If a scheduling conflict arises between a quinceañera and a wedding, will the quinceañera reservation be honored?
- What the fee for the church is and what it includes. When must it be paid? Can the fee be paid in installments? Under what circumstances will the church refund the fee?
- Whether the quinceañera is required to work in the community or at the church as part of her preparation.

All of these details should be raised during your meeting with the priest or minister, an appointment for which should be made as soon as you decide to have a celebration. Whatever the requirements are, they are often strictly enforced. One girl in San Antonio missed most of the preparation classes because of illness in her family. She lost her $200 deposit and ended up having her celebration at a later date in another church. As soon as you decide to have a quinceañera celebration, reserve the church and talk with the pastor to find out what is required of you and your family and whether they can celebrate the religious service you want.

The Spiritual Preparation

Most churches, regardless of denomination, require the quinceañera to go through spiritual preparation, whether it's a couple of meetings with the minister or priest or a year of religion classes. The preparation helps the quinceañera understand why the church service is an important element of her celebration.

The church service is a celebration of thanksgiving. The girl thanks God for her fifteen years on earth, for the love and protection of her family, for the blessings she has received in her young life. The parents thank God for giving them their daughter and keeping her with them for fifteen years, for the blessings He has bestowed on them through her, for protecting her and keeping her from harm. The family thanks God for bestowing the girl on them, for her sweetness and humor, for her goodness and intelligence.

The preparation classes challenge the quinceañera and the members of her court, who are also often required to attend classes or a retreat, to examine their ideas and beliefs and discover their strengths. After the teens reflect on their lives and their values, they come away with a better appreciation of the changes that are going on in them and around them. "So that it really becomes a rite of passage, a bridge moment that they can come back to in their lives and mine out the gold that they've experienced," said the Reverend Arturo Perez, who headed the quinceañera preparation program at St. Roman Church.

Years ago, when the quinceañera celebration was code to announce a girl was on the marriage market, her preparation was limited to the skills that would help her make a home for her family—cooking, cleaning, ironing, caring for children, sewing. Just as the meaning of the tradition has changed, so has the preparation. Today this preparation gives the clergy and lay teachers a chance to discuss the sacredness of the quinceañera's life, the sacredness of womanhood, and her responsibility to herself. "It allows us to talk about sexuality in real positive terms before everybody," said Father Perez. "It gives us an opportunity to say to her and the girls in her court, 'You hold power in this community.' Because that's what sexuality is about, in a lot of ways. How will they use it? For good? Or not for good?"

Before 1989, La Rabaña Church in Chicago rejected the idea of celebrating quince años. "We looked at it as a worldly thing, as little more than a party, and this was a no-no. This is what our evangelical teaching was," said the Reverend Ruth Mercado, a co-pastor of the church.

One of their parishioners, Enit Negrón, convinced the pastors that the celebration was a way to strengthen the relationship between a girl and her parents, a way to help teenage girls get through the rough spots in their young lives. "When they turn fifteen, it is an age when many teens lose themselves, they change direction. But when they are baptized and they remember God in their youth, it's a little easier," said Negrón.

The celebration that Negrón created for her daughter, Millie, was an homage. She highlighted the accomplishments Millie had achieved with God's grace in her fifteen years, everything from taking her first steps and cutting her first tooth to her spiritual and educational achievements. "When we saw this mother and the way she did it, and how special her daughter felt, we thought it was a good thing to do," said Mercado.

Now the quinceañero is very much a part of La Rabaña Church. Parishioners who have experience planning and producing a quinceañero make up a committee to help the family create the celebration, from the service to the party afterward.

Marisela Martinez had her quinceañera celebration at

Lisa Alfaro of Chicago stands on the threshold of her home and adolescence. With her younger sister Lillian at her side and her best friend, Elizabeth Martinez—her maid of honor—standing behind her, they get ready to walk to the church to celebrate Lisa's coming of age.
—Salvador Hernandez

Chicago's Our Lady of Tepeyac, which requires the quinceañeras to attend ten weeks of classes and to craft their own ceremony. Marisela's mother, Susana, said that the preparation process strengthened her relationship with both her daughters.

"You have to plan the first reading, the second reading, the gospel—you get to pick your own mass," said Susana Martinez. "They gave us three or four readings to choose from, and Marisela would read them to me and I would read them to her so we could hear how they would sound. My oldest daughter, Julie, helped us a lot. I think that's what's made us closer, all three of us. Because Julie was really involved in planning the mass *también.*"

The Church Ceremony

THE PROCESSIONAL

Across the main aisle at the First Congregational Church in Danbury, where the Hispanic United Church of Christ holds their services, a gold and white ribbon stretched across the threshold that Jacqueline Delao was about to cross. When the music started and the court began to file

---

Some of the Spiritual Questions Asked at St. Pius and St. Roman

• What responsibilities do you have in your home? Doing the dinner dishes? Keeping your room clean? Running errands for your parents?

• What passages have you already had in life, such as changing from middle to high school? How did you feel about the changes?

• Of all the festivities during that day, what is the most important hour you are going to pass?

• Why are you having a mass to celebrate your fifteenth birthday?

• Why is it important to bring the family together for your celebration?

• What are your moral values? Honesty? Loyalty? What others?

• What do you want to do with your life? What do you see in your future? What are your goals?

• What career do you dream of?

• How is your communication with your parents? Good? Bad? Do you communicate at all?

• What do you like about being part of the Catholic Church, and what don't you like?

• What do you see as your role in the Church?

• How will you live the commitment you make when you renew your baptismal vows?

• Once you've had your quinceañera, will you act more mature? Will you be a person of your word?

in, the first young girl, one of three among the court, stepped onto the red carpet carrying a white basket. When she reached the barrier, she pulled a gleaming pair of silver shears from the basket and cut the ribbon, symbolizing Jackie's entrance into adolescence before God and her community of family and friends.

Sometimes a church has a prescribed order for the entrance; sometimes the pastor will make suggestions, but lets the family decide who and how everyone should enter. Traditionally the quinceañera comes in last, with her guests, her family, and whoever preceded her in the processional gathered to receive her in the next phase of her life. Sometimes she walks in with her parents, sometimes with one parent or the other, sometimes alone, depending on the custom of the church and the family. Many clergy frown on the girl walking into—and sometimes even out of—the church with her boyfriend, saying it adds to the confusion with a wedding.

If gifts are to be blessed as part of a Catholic ceremony, they should be carried in during the processional, not the offertory, according to Sister Rosa Maria Icazas. The Church leaves the specific gifts to be given to the discretion of the families and the individual parishes. "These are what we call popular expressions of faith, and therefore nothing is dictated. None of the gifts are dictated," said Icazas.

THE SERVICE

Depending on the denomination and the clergy at a particular church, the quinceañera may have a lot of input into crafting a service or she may simply decide who will participate. Some of these elements may be included:

- Members of her family and the court are often asked to do the readings. Your pastor will often suggest Scripture passages, or you might choose the ones from the list that starts on page 46. Choose readings that have meaning for you. You may want to discuss your selections with your pastor before making a final decision.
- The padrinos for the church, for baptism, for the Virgin's bouquet of red roses, the medal, the ring, the book, that rosary, and any other gift walk their offering to the

altar to be blessed and present it to the quinceañera during the mass. In a Protestant service, the quinceañera may be presented with a bouquet of red roses. Someone may read the symbolism of each gift as it is presented.

- The quinceañera herself, an example to young people, may be asked to write her own prayer, thanking God for her blessings and asking him for his help in the future.

- The parents may be asked to stand in front of the congregation to tell the congregation what they are thankful for.

- Sometimes the godparents sit on the altar with the quinceañera.

- The priest or minister gives the quinceañera a sign of peace, who gives it to her parents, and from there it slowly spreads through the church.

- The quinceañera renews her baptismal vows.

- The quinceañera may light her baptismal candle or another candle on the altar. In a candlelight ceremony, the congregation all hold candles. After the quinceañera lights her baptismal candle, she lights her parents' candles, who light their parents' candles, and so on until everyone holds a lit candle, a symbol of the quinceañera sharing the spiritual light within her.

- The quinceañera may make a public commitment to her family, her faith, her education, and her chastity.

- Changing the quinceañera's shoes from flats to heels signifies her transition from a girl to a young woman. A Puerto Rican custom calls for the priest to bless the heels and her crown. Her father changes her shoes while she is sitting at the altar, and then her mother places the crown on her head.

- In some Central American countries, the quinceañera walks into the church carrying a doll, which symbolizes her entrance into the church as a child. During the service, she exchanges the doll for a rosary and prayer book or a Bible. The gesture is a way of expressing the idea of leaving childish things behind and taking up the Word of God.

- The parents may bless the daughter, or the entire congregation may bless the quinceañera along with the minister before the recessional.

READINGS

Although the Bible does not specifically mention quince años celebrations, it does have a wealth of things to say about youth, respecting one's parents, and thanksgiving. The readings and reflections incorporated into the service should be based on the Bible, many theologians advise. Some denominations incorporate only one passage, some more; some specify the text must come from the New Testament, others from the Old Testament. Your pastor will tell you how many selections you'll need to make, where they'll come in the service, and whether a member of the ministry will read them or whether you can choose a friend or relative to read a Bible passage you select.

The readings incorporate the Word of God into the service to inspire not only the quinceañera but her family and friends gathered in the church. The passages celebrate her spiritual maturity and help her define her role in the church, her changing status in her family, and her responsibilities to the community. Here are some suggestions for you to consider and to discuss with your pastor.

❧ Colossians 3:12–17	Forgive one another and give thanks
❧ I Corinthians 13:1–7	Love is patient
❧ 2 Corinthians 6:16	I will be their God
❧ Deuteronomy 6:1–2, 4–6, 5:16	Honor your parents
❧ Ecclesiastes 12:1	Remember now thy Creator
❧ Ephesians 4:1–6	One God and Father of all
❧ Galatians 3:27–29	All one in Christ
❧ Isaiah 32:1–9	Here is my servant
❧ Isaiah 43:1–7	I have called you by name
❧ Isaiah 44:1–8	I am the Lord's
❧ Isaiah 49:1–7	The Lord called me from birth
❧ Jeremiah 1:4–10	Jeremiah is called

§ John 4:1–11   Jesus meets the woman at the well

§ John 4:7–21   God is love

§ Luke 2:41–52   Jesus among the elders

§ 1 Peter 1:13–21   Be holy, for I am holy

§ 2 Peter 1:3–11   Christian virtue

§ 2 Peter 1:12–19   Witness to Christ

§ Psalm 100:2–3   Serve the Lord with gladness

§ Psalm 116   I love the Lord

§ Psalm 119:9   Where shall a young man cleanse his way?

§ Psalm 145   David's psalm of praise

§ Psalm 149   Sing a new song

§ 1 Samuel 3:1–21   The Lord calls Samuel

§ 2 Timothy 1:3–14   I give thanks to God

You may also be asked to select the Gospel passage the priest or minister reads. Here are some suggestions for you to consider.

§ John 7:37–39   Streams of living water

§ John 10:7–18   I am the Good Shepherd

§ John 12:20–28   The grain of wheat

§ John 15:1–17   The vine and the branches

§ John 17:1–8   Father, the hour has come

§ John 17:9–26   I pray for them

§ Luke 1:26–38   Mary is called

§ Luke 1:46–55   Mary's song of praise

§ Luke 2:22–35   Jesus' presentation in the temple

§ Luke 2:41–52 — The finding in the temple

§ Luke 8:1–3 — The women follow Jesus

§ Luke 10:38–42 — Mary and Martha

§ Luke 15:8–10 — Joy at finding the lost

§ Mark 4:35–41 — Jesus calms a storm

§ Mark 6:45–52 — Jesus walks on the water

§ Mark 10:13–16 — Jesus blesses little children

§ Mark 10:17–31 — The rich young man

§ Matthew 1:18–23 — The birth of Jesus Christ

§ Matthew 3:13–17 — The baptism of Jesus

§ Matthew 5:13–16 — The salt of the earth and light of the world

§ Matthew 6:19–34 — Seek first the kingdom of God

§ Matthew 11:25–30 — Come to me

§ § *Don't Forget the Family Traditions* § §

Lillian Alfaro turned three years old around the time her older sister Lisa turned fifteen. Their parents, Leslie and Graciela, keep a family tradition of presenting a child at church around her third birthday. The priest invites the child up to the altar, and he or she recites a prayer. The Alfaros combined the two ceremonies into one, and Lillian, one of the two flower girls in Lisa's court, made her presentation during Lisa's quinceañera. She recited the Lord's Prayer.

MUSIC

Five years before her quinceañera, Benita Arevalo's grandmother died. Benita and her grandmother had enjoyed a close relationship, and Benita would often visit her after school. On weekends they would see each other: either Benita and her family would visit her grandmother or she would come to Benita's house. Her grandmother had urged her to have a quinceañera celebration.

As Benita, her mother, and her sister planned her quinceañera, they wanted to honor her grandmother, to make her memory part of the celebration. They decided to include two of her grandmother's favorite songs as part of the mass, and asked Benita's choir teacher to sing them.

These are some of the music pieces quinceañeras around the country choose for their services: Dominique Estell Chavez, who is Lutheran, had these hymns:

*   "Borning Cry"
*   "Let All Mortal Flesh Keep Silence"
*   "Ave Maria"
*   "Amazing Grace"

Demaris Carolina Vasquez had these hymns at her Lutheran service:

*   "De Colores"
*   "Tú Has Venido a la Orilla"
*   "Yo Tengo Fe"

At Lisa Alfaro's Catholic mass, there was this music:

*   "Ode to Joy" from Beethoven's Ninth Symphony
*   "Feliz Quinceañera"
*   "Quinceañera" by Juanita Villastrigo
*   "Virgencita" by Carlos Rosas
*   "Las Mañanitas"

THE RECESSIONAL

At the end of the mass, Father Frank Macías turned to the guests gathered at San Fernando Cathedral to introduce la señorita who stood next to him. "And now it is my pleasure, my pride, my little sister, to present to the whole world, Celia Marie Hernandez." With that, she was free to march into the world and celebrate. Celia's recessional was very simple: the court walked out of the church in the same order they walked in.

Just as some people choose to emphasize the processional into the church, others prefer to accent the exit with an archway. Bouquets, canes, sabers, hats, parasols, ribbons, and hands, whatever the court holds is raised in the air to form an archway, to symbolize their support for the quinceañera's passage from God's house into the world.

At Jackie Delao's celebration, the boys and girls who stood with her left their seats, each couple meeting at the center aisle. There they formed two lines. When Jackie left, the girls held up their roses and the boys their white-tipped canes to form an arch, through which Jackie and her father, followed by her mother on the arm of the honor escort, walked out into the world.

Generally the court walks out in the same order they walked in, but the quinceañera has a choice. She can walk out with her parents or with her escort.

At St. Roman Church in Chicago, the quinceañera walked in with her parents, but left with her chambelán de honor, as a way of highlighting her change in status. "That ritualizes more the idea that she is moving into another stage now," said Father Perez. "She comes in with her parents, but she leaves with this young man."

❧ ❧ *Where There Are Hispanics, There Are Quinceañeras* ❧ ❧

Carmen Martinez grew up in San Antonio, a devout Catholic. Her family did not have the money to have a quinceañera for her, and she was unable to have one for her daughter. She insisted, however, that her granddaughter, Dominique Chavez, have as grand and traditional a celebration as the family could afford, including a mass. But years before Dominique's fifteenth birthday drew near, her family left the Catholic Church and converted to Lutheranism. The Chavezes worked with their pastor, the Reverend Marilyn Galloway Lange, to craft a quinceañera ceremony that reflected their religion. Dominique's was the first quinceañera celebration in the Hosanna! Lutheran congregation. "To me, having the mass in a Lutheran church was different, but I thought it would be beautiful," Carmen Martinez said. "It gives people a chance to see that not only Catholics can have a quinceañera. It's just one Lord, one God for all of us."

Chapter Four

A Ball in Your Honor: The Reception

The celebration starts with the show. And from there, a party—with food, open bar, you name it. A *party*.

—*Juan Muñoz, Fort Lauderdale, Florida*

Inside the glass doors at the Tropigala Banquet Hall, hints of the evening's delights could be seen. On a white napped and skirted table, ceramic carousel horses stood waiting to deliver place cards to each guest. From a 16-by-20-inch portrait, the quinceañera greeted her guests with a smile. A life-size carousel horse drew the guests into the main room.

Inside, a table laden with hors d'oeuvres stretched along two walls. On each table arranged around the dance floor pranced a plumed carousel horse. Around the center-pieces, beautiful place settings with a treasure trove of favors and decorations awaited the guests.

But it would be the parquet dance floor and the stage, set with a carousel, two foun-tains, and two beautiful flower arrangements of pink and white carnations that would

FACING PAGE: *Vicente Villalobo waltzes with his daughter, Alicia, at her* quinces *celebration in Miami. The waltz is usually the first dance in the choreography, a series of dances performed by the court of honor and the quinceañera gen-erally following the presentation. Mexicans generally dance four numbers, but Cubans and other Caribbean Latinos may dance eight or more.* —Enrique Muñoz Studio

command attention. From behind that carousel, on that stage would emerge the focus of the evening, the reason that everyone had gathered from as far away as New Jersey: Teresita Perez, la quinceañera.

The reception is the moment you have dreamt about, waited, worked and planned for. La fiesta. The party. Your presentation. A well-planned reception will bring together all those elements you will be shopping for and working on and rehearsing into one enchanted evening. Think of the reception as having four major parts: the guests' arrival, the dinner, the presentation, and the dance. This order is not cast in stone. In some parts of the country, the presentation follows the guests' arrival. The dinner and dance become the quinceañera's first social appearance as a young lady. In other areas of the country, however, the order is reversed. The guests eat earlier in the evening, when the quinceañera is still *una niña*, but she attends the dance as *una señorita*.

In your notebook of dreams, write down a schedule, indicating when and where you want the other elements—the thank-you, the cutting of the cake, the last doll. At least a week before the party you will need to check with everyone you have hired to confirm they will be coming and to make sure everything they need at the site is available for them.

The Reception Site

Now that you have an idea of the kind of quinceañera you want—your colors, your theme, the style—you are ready to look for the setting in which you will have your party. The reception, whether it's held at a hotel ballroom, a country club, a banquet hall, a church basement or on a yacht, will take the biggest bite out of your budget.

The first decision to make is whether you are simply looking for a place to hold the party or for a place that will provide the food, drinks, decorations and sometimes even the music as well.

Reception sites can be in demand, especially in the spring and summer and during the Christmas party season. Most banquet-hall managers and caterers say they will take reservations with just a few days' notice if the date is free. But why take the chance? The sooner you reserve their services and put down a deposit, the more likely you will get

❧ ❧ *A Sample Reception Schedule* ❧ ❧

A quinceañera reception—the dinner and dance—typically runs between four and six hours. You might want to schedule a six-hour reception, from 6 P.M. to midnight, something like this:

6 P.M.	The guests arrive
6 P.M. to 7 P.M.	Social or cocktail hour with any entertainment you may have planned
7 P.M. to 8 P.M.	Dinner with more of the same entertainment, or new entertainment
8 P.M. to 9 P.M.	The march or choreography, presentation and waltz, toast, thank-you
9 P.M. to 10 P.M.	Dance
10 P.M. to 10:15 P.M.	Present the quinceañera with her last doll; everyone sings happy birthday; cut the cake
10:15 P.M. to 12 midnight	Dance
12 midnight	Party ends, guests leave

what you want when you want it. At the same time, don't rush into signing a contract before you know exactly what you want and will need.

If you live in an area where many banquet halls, public and private country clubs, restaurants, and hotels compete for banquet business, you may find managers more willing to negotiate. Below are some suggestions for dealing with the site manager. Remember, the more guests you are planning to have, the more food the caterer has to order. Buying the larger quantities enables the caterer to get better prices from his or her suppliers. Negotiating will get some of those savings passed on to you.

Some places, like Angelito's Banquet Hall in Hialeah, Florida, and Tania's in

§ § *Questions for the Reception Site Manager* § §

• How many people does the room hold?

• How much is the rental fee, and what exactly does it include? Kitchen facilities? Cleanup? Security? Rehearsal?

• What kind of deposit is required? Under what conditions is it refunded?

• What are the payment terms?

• Is there an escalation clause if I book in advance? (If there is, try to negotiate a ceiling.)

• What is the charge for additional time if the party runs long?

• Do I have to guarantee a minimum number of guests?

• How many events are going on at once?

• How do you ensure privacy?

• Is the dance floor extra?

• Is there a coat check?

• What facilities are there for a band or DJ? Are microphones available? Are there restrictions on the music?

• What kind of electrical outlets are available?

• Are there any restrictions on the caterer I use?

• What kind of parking is available? Do you offer valet parking?

• Does this location have liability insurance in case a guest is injured or there is a DWI accident by someone leaving the party?

• When can the court come in for rehearsal?

• When can the family or outside florist come in to decorate?

• Who is hired as security—off-duty police officers in uniform or private security guards?

The answers to all those questions should appear in the contract. If the reception site is providing the music, choreographer, catering, or any other service, the details for those services need to be specified in writing as well.

Chicago, can help you put together a comprehensive package, from the decorations and food to the music and choreography. "We do everything except the invitations," said Nivaldo Cruz, Angelito's president. They even have a Cinderella pumpkin coach available to rent for the presentation!

You will save money in a banquet hall, but your celebration may have more atmosphere at a country club. "In a banquet hall, you have your set menus, and usually the food is not made on the premises," said Lizy Hernandez, the Miami party planner. "In a country club, you're able to meet the chef and talk over with him or her what you would like. You can personalize the menu."

The Key to a Good Party: Food and Refreshments

What is the key to a good party? For some it's what they wear, for others it's the music. But Angelito's Nivaldo Cruz says the secret of success is in the eats: "To me an event is judged by the food."

When quinceañeras were held at home back in our native lands, the menus were much more narrowly defined. Often we made the food ourselves. But as we become more assimilated and achieve more economic success, our tastes change. The chef at a catering hall or a country club that we have fallen in love with for the reception may not know how to prepare *comida típica*, popular dishes from our cultures. And they may not be the quinceañera's favorite food anyway. It's as common to find chicken Kiev served at a Cuban quinces in Miami as it is to find Polish sausage served at a Mexican celebration in Chicago. The important thing is to think of a menu that will not only satisfy you and your guests but will contribute to the air of celebration.

Are you going to have the party catered? Or are you and your family and friends going to make the food yourself? Are you going to have a sit-down dinner served in courses? Or do you prefer a buffet?

You'll save money by making the food yourself, but unless you are very well organized and have a posse of relatives and friends to help, the logistics and sheer amount of work can leave you exhausted and frazzled on the day you should enjoy most. The brother of Sarah Arevalo's boss owned a renowned tamale business in San Antonio and promised her all the tamales she wanted. "I had my best friend make the potato salad, the rice, and the beans," said Arevalo. But on the day of the quinceañera, on top of all the countless last-minute details to attend to, the Arevalos had to pick up the tamales for several hundred people and arrived late for the mass. By asking a reliable friend or family member to take charge of the food, the Arevalos would have had fewer things to take care of that day, and the person who coordinated the food would have made an invaluable contribution to Benita's quinces.

How long the evening lasts will also determine when and how much food is served. If an elaborately choreographed event will take place before dinner, you may want to have a lot of hors d'oeuvres on hand during the social hour to tide the guests over until the main meal is served.

Menu Suggestions

A CUBAN SIT-DOWN QUINCES DINNER

Various hot and cold hors d'oeuvres

Selection of fruit and cheese

Selection of breads and crackers

Jigote (chicken consommé)

Carne mechada (stuffed *boliche*, a cut of beef from the thigh)

Arroz (rice)

Tostones (fried plantains)

Yucca

Cake

Coffee

Dessert tray—cakes, petit fours, berries and cream, mousse, ice cream, cookies, tiny tarts

Jigote

This delicate consommé is traditionally served in bouillon cups to guests to signal the start of an elegant buffet. It is equally appropriate at a sit-down dinner.

1 chicken (4 to 5 pounds)
3 pounds beef
2-3 veal bones
4 quarts water
2 carrots
2 small turnips
1 stalk celery with leaves
1 large onion, stuck with 2 cloves

1 clove garlic
1 bay leaf
2-3 sprigs parsley
salt and fresh ground pepper
½ teaspoon allspice
1 cup dry sherry

In a large soup kettle, place all the meat and bones, including the chicken giblets. Add the water and bring to a simmer. Skim all the fat and scum as it rises. Do not let the broth boil, or it will become cloudy. When there is nothing left to skim, cover the pot and cook for three hours.

Add all the remaining ingredients except the sherry. Return the broth to a simmer and cook slowly for another two hours. Strain the broth, which will have been reduced to about three quarts. Cool to room temperature before refrigerating overnight.

The next day, skim any fat from the broth's surface. Remove the chicken breast, gizzard, and liver from the broth. Line a sieve with several layers of dampened cheesecloth or a napkin. Pour the broth through the sieve and into a saucepan to strain out any remaining particles of fat. Add the sherry to the broth and heat through.

While the broth and sherry heat, grind the reserved cooked meats together. When ready to serve, place a teaspoon of the ground meats in the bottom of each bouillon cup before adding the hot consommé.

Serves 12

A Mexican Quinceañera Buffet Menu

Guacamole (avocado sauce)

Pico de gallo (fresh tomato, onion, and cilantro relish)

Tostaditos (tortilla chips)

Mole poblano (turkey in mole sauce)

Frijoles refritos (refried beans)

A relish of jalapeños, carrots, and onions

Arroz (rice)

Tamales

Ensalada mixta (mixed salad)

Pastel (cake)

Jarascas (cookies)

Mole Poblano

According to legend, the good nuns in the convent of Santa Rosa first served this dish to a visiting viceroy and archbishop. But it was the Indian girls who gave this royal recipe, the most famous of all moles, to the nuns.

6 *ancho* chilies

6 *pasilla* chilies

6 *mulato* chilies

1 turkey (8 pounds), cut into serving pieces (reserve the giblets)

4–8 tablespoons lard

1 carrot, sliced

2 onions, chopped

4 whole cloves garlic

Salt and fresh ground pepper to taste

½ teaspoon anise

4 tablespoons sesame seeds

1 cup whole blanched almonds

½ teaspoon ground cloves

½ teaspoon ground cinnamon

½ teaspoon ground coriander

I tortilla

½ cup raisins

3 sprigs fresh coriander

I pound tomatoes, seeded

1½ ounces unsweetened chocolate

If you are using dried chilies, slit them open and remove the veins and seeds. Save at least I tablespoon of seeds. Put the chilies in a bowl, covering them with three cups of hot water, for I to 2 hours.

While the chilies soak, brown the turkey in the lard. Pour off and reserve the excess fat. Cover the pan and braise the turkey until tender, about 60 minutes. You can do this on top of the stove or in an oven preheated to 325 degrees.

While the turkey is cooking, place the turkey giblets, the carrot, one of the onions, and one clove of garlic in a saucepan. Cover with water and season with salt and fresh ground pepper to taste. Simmer for I½ hours. Strain, cool, and set aside.

When the turkey is cooked, drain the juices from the pan and set the meat aside. Skim the fat from the juice. Add the juices to the broth. Reduce the broth to two cups. Set aside.

Put the chilies and their water into a blender and process until smooth. In a heated frying pan, combine the remaining 3 whole cloves of garlic, the anise seeds, ½ the sesame seeds, the chili seeds, and the almonds. Toast them, stirring constantly until lightly browned. Add the ground spices and heat until they release their fragrance. Let cool and put the mixture in a blender jar. Reheat the lard, and fry the tortilla until very crisp. Crumble and add to the blender jar. Sauté the raisins in the hot fat until they swell up. Remove the raisins to paper toweling to absorb the fat. Add the raisins, the remaining onion, the fresh coriander, and the tomatoes to the blender jar and puree to a smooth paste. Fry the paste in the hot lard for 10 minutes, stirring constantly. Be prepared for spatters.

Add the chocolate to the puree and cook until the chocolate melts, taking care the chocolate does not burn. Add the turkey broth and salt and pepper to taste and cook over low heat until the sauce becomes thicker than heavy cream, at least 40 minutes.

Add the turkey to the sauce and cook over very low heat another 20 to 30 minutes, until the flavors of the meat and sauce blend. Sprinkle with the remaining sesame seeds.

Serves 8 to 10

A Puerto Rican Feast

Pastelillos de carne de cerdo (little pork pies)

Lechón (roast suckling pig) with *ajilimójili* (garlic and pepper sauce)

Pollo asado a la criolla (roasted chicken creole)

Arroz con gandules (rice and pigeon peas)

Mollejitas en escabeche (pickled chicken gizzards)

Potato salad

Tostones (fried plantains)

Piononos (plantains stuffed with beef)

Pastelillos de Cerdo

These little pork pies, the Puerto Rican version of empanadas, are delicious. Serve them as canapés or appetizers, depending on their size.

The Pastry

2 cups all-purpose flour

I teaspoon salt

½ teaspoon baking soda

4 tablespoons unsalted butter

I egg, slightly beaten, with ½ cup water

Sift the dry ingredients together into a large bowl. Cut in the butter, combining to the consistency of coarse meal. Pour the egg and water into the center of the flour. Mix until dough is smooth and forms a ball. Wrap the dough in wax paper and refrigerate for I hour.

The Filling

½ pound ground lean pork

⅛ pound ground ham

3 tablespoons lard or oil

1 cup *sofrito* (see below)

2 teaspoons white vinegar

2 teaspoons capers

2 teaspoons raisins

¼ cup small green olives, pitted

1 hard-boiled egg, chopped

Sauté the meat in the oil or lard, seasoning it with salt and fresh ground pepper, until the meat is brown. Add the *sofrito* and vinegar, combine well, and cook for 30 minutes over low heat. Add the remaining ingredients and cook for another two minutes. Set aside to cool.

Divide the dough into thirds. Working with each third at a time, roll onto a lightly floured board to ⅛-inch thickness. Cut the dough into 4-inch circles for appetizers or 2½-inch circles for canapés. In the larger circle, place 1 tablespoon of the meat mixture; 1 teaspoon of the meat in the smaller circles. Moisten the edge of the dough with cold water, fold the dough in half and pinch the pie closed. Press the edges with the tines of a fork to seal.

Heat oil in a deep fat fryer to 350 degrees. Fry the little pies until they float to the top. Spoon a bit of the hot oil over them so they puff up. Fry until brown. Drain on paper towels.

Or to bake them, heat the oven to 350 degrees. Place the little pies on baking sheets lined with parchment paper. Bake until golden brown, about 20 minutes.

Makes 18 larger pies or 4 dozen smaller ones

Sofrito

2 medium onions	¼ pound diced ham
6 cloves garlic	1 tablespoon chopped fresh cilantro
1 green pepper	1 teaspoon dried oregano
½ pound tomatoes	Salt and fresh ground pepper to taste
¼ pound diced salt pork	
1 tablespoon achiote (annatto) seeds	

Finely chop the onions, garlic, and green pepper. Peel, seed, and chop the tomatoes.

Fry the salt pork until it will render no more fat and the meat is crisp and golden. Remove the dice from the fat and drain on paper towels. In the hot fat that remains, sauté the achiote for five minutes. The fat will be a beautiful red. Strain the fat and discard the seeds, returning the fat to the pan.

Sauté the onions, garlic, and green pepper until the onion is translucent. Add the remaining ingredients and simmer over low heat for 30 minutes, stirring occasionally.

Makes about 1 cup

DOMINICAN FAVORITES

Lechón con mojo (roast suckling pig with scallion sauce)

Arroz con camarones (shrimp and rice)

Serenata (salt codfish salad)

Pastel de mapueyes (yam pie)

Rice

Bizcocho (cake)

Coffee

Lechón

Throughout the Spanish-speaking countries of the Caribbean, momentous occasions are marked with lechón, roast suckling pig. Traditionally barbecued over a wood fire, many a succulent lechón has been cooked in ovens of city apartments. Each culture has its favorite sauce to serve with the pig. Some suggestions follow.

The Marinade

I medium onion, finely chopped
I head garlic, peeled and finely chopped
2 tablespoons dried oregano
2 tablespoons salt

I tablespoon freshly ground pepper
I cup Seville (bitter) orange juice, or
 I cup lime juice

Mix the ingredients. Baste the pig inside and out with the marinade, leaving the meat to season overnight. Turn and baste the meat every few hours.

The Pig

I suckling pig (10 to 12 pounds),
 cleaned and oven-ready
Salt

Marinade
¼ cup vegetable oil or butter

Wash the pig in cold water and pat dry. Season inside and out with salt and the marinade. Let it rest overnight in the marinade, turning it once or twice and basting the inside with the liquid.

When ready to roast, heat the oven to 325 degrees. Crumple aluminum foil into a ball the size of whatever you plan to place in the pig's mouth on the serving platter—an apple, an orange, a lime, for example. Place the ball inside the pig's mouth. Pull the rear legs back and tie with string. Pull the front legs forward and tie with string. Place the pig on a rack in a large roasting pan. Pour the marinade over the pig. Cover the pig with foil and roast in the oven for 2½ hours. Every half hour, baste the meat with the marinade and the juices from the bottom of the roasting pan. Remove the foil and roast for another 30 minutes, until the pig turns a golden brown. Baste frequently during the last half hour. The pig is done when the juices that run from a knife-prick in the thigh run clear or a meat thermometer inserted in the thigh registers 170 degrees.

Place the pig on a platter and replace the foil ball in its mouth. Let the meat rest 10 to 15 minutes before carving.

Ajilimójili
Puerto Rican Garlic and Pepper Sauce for Lechón

3 fresh hot red peppers
3 fresh sweet red peppers
6 cloves garlic
8 peppercorns

½ cup lime juice, or ¼ cup lime juice and
 ¼ cup vinegar
½ cup vegetable oil, preferably olive oil

Remove the veins and seeds from the peppers. Peel the garlic. Place all ingredients in a blender and purée.

Makes 3 cups

Mojo para Lechón
Sauce for Roast Suckling Pig from the Dominican Republic

8 cloves garlic
½ cup scallions
⅔ cup peanut oil
1 teaspoon fresh hot pepper

½ cup cane or malt vinegar
½ cup Seville (bitter) orange juice
Salt and pepper to taste

Peel the garlic and finely chop the cloves with the scallions. Sauté them in the oil until translucent. Add the rest of the ingredients, cooking for two to three minutes until the flavors are blended. Serve with the *lechón*.

Makes 2 cups

Finding a Caterer

Sometimes you can use only the caterer that works with a specific reception site. But other times, who makes the food you will serve is up to you. Here are some suggestions to help you start your hunt:

- Try word of mouth. Ask other people who have organized quinceañeras to recommend caterers they considered, or better still, used. Other sources for recommendations are a party planner, the seamstress who is making the dress, the choreographer, even the quinceañera coordinator at your church.
- Check the yellow pages. You'll find plenty of suggestions there.
- Ask at restaurants. Often your favorite restaurant or its chef will cater parties.
- Consider your local bodegas. If your neighborhood grocery store serves prepared food, chances are they may also cater parties. Talk with the owner or the manager.

Keep track of your contacts in your notebook, noting what each one's specialty is, the cost, and what besides food they provide. How is the meal served and by whom? Are the platters garnished? Will the caterer take care of ordering plates, glassware, flatware, and linens if the reception site manager does not?

Ask the caterer for references from people who have hired him or her, as well as the last three places where she or he has catered an event. Has the caterer done a quinceañera before? Ask him or her to describe the meal.

If you have a particular dish you want served, ask if the caterer knows how to make it and make sure, through your discussion, that he or she does. Ask for samples of dishes they serve. This is especially important if the caterer does not come recommended from anyone whose judgment you trust or if you've never tasted his or her wares.

❧ ❧ Questions to Ask When You Meet with the Caterer ❧ ❧ and Areas to Specify in the Contract

• Date, time, and where the reception will be catered

• The cost per plate. Does this include taxes and tips?

• The number of people you expect to attend

• Are there any extra or hidden charges? Is there a service charge for cutting and serving the cake if I bring in my own?

• The charge for the bar, and the time it will open and close

• A detailed menu that includes your selections for each course or buffet station

• Rental fees, if any, for linens, china, glass are, and flatware, and how many of each item

• The number of hors d'oeuvres and canapés you are ordering (avoid buying by the tray;

you do not know precisely what you are get ing for your money)

• The cost of extras

• The deposit, payment schedule, and accept ble forms of payment; conditions under hich you can get a refund

• The price for the food and beverage service and what exactly it includes.

• The ratio of guests to service staff (1 to 12 is considered adequate for sit-down diners; 1 to 15 or 18 for buffets)

• The kind of serving dishes that will be used—stainless, copper, or silver plate?

• The garnishes on the platters

• Will each table be cleared before dessert is served? Will coffee be served with dessert? or a buffet, will plates be cleared away when guest returns to the buffet?

The answers to these questions and any others you may have should be incorporated into the contract.

The Guests Arrive

The way your guests are greeted at the door of your reception sets the tone for the whole party. The area may be decorated with streamers, balloons, flowers—whatever suits your theme, your taste, and the ambiance you want to create. Framed photos of the quinceañera or a collage of her photos through the years are a nice touch. If you have had a large formal portrait done of her in her dress, this is the place to display it. For the place cards and the guest book—for whatever you want in the entryway—you will need a table near the door large enough to accommodate everything you want to display.

Asking guests to sign the mat around the portrait is an increasingly popular alternative to the guest book. If you prefer to keep the mat untouched, keep a guest book and pen on the table, as well as the place cards arranged alphabetically, if you have assigned specific tables to specific families.

Depending on the number of favors you plan to give your guests, you may want to greet them with a souvenir. Ana Maria Valenzuela made 300 tiny white rosaries decorated with rosebuds and tiny leaves from *migajón de pan,* a malleable sort of clay made from white bread and glue, for the guests who came to daughter Laura's quinceañera. Each was slipped into its own plastic bag and tucked inside a small basket Laura had decorated with pink and white yarn. Laura stood at the door, greeting each of her guests with the tiny basket and a capia, and asked each to sign her guest book.

A WORD ABOUT SECURITY

Unfortunately, we live in uncertain times. Who actually comes to the celebration is often as big a concern as whom we invite. While Latinos from Cuba to Chile traditionally made friendships not just with individuals but with their families, that custom is harder to maintain as we move to large cities or the suburbs. Tradition calls for us to know the parents of our children's friends, but oftentimes we do not. As our celebrations become more formal and we turn to caterers for our feasts, we must keep as close an eye on the number of guests who come as we do on their relationship to us. This can defuse confrontations and keep them from escalating into dangerous scenes.

The Social Hour

Is a cocktail hour appropriate at a quinceañera? That depends on whether you view the occasion as a party for a girl and her friends or for adults to honor a young woman. A span of time at the beginning, before the choreography begins or dinner is served, will allow your guests to find their seats, to get to know one another, and to admire the decoration of the room that you've so painstakingly planned and carried out.

Entertainment—strolling musicians, mariachis, or the disc jockey playing background music—can entice people into the room and make them feel more welcome, more at home. It can set the tone of the party to come.

Whether or not you decide to serve alcohol is entirely up to you. An open bar is most expensive, with the caterer or reception site manager charging a set price per drink, which is negotiated with the contract. Or you may decide to simply serve beer and wine. Rolando and Esther Nieto decided to compromise at their daughter Michele's celebration. Because Esther and her family are Baptists, they do not drink alcohol. But Rolando knew that his side of the family would expect some sort of libation. They decided to put one bottle of liquor in a beautifully decorated basket on each table. The waiters would bring the ice and mixers and even mix the drinks, but when the bottle at the table was empty, that was all the liquor available. And the baskets that held the bottles were among the items the guests took home with them.

Make sure there are plenty of soft drinks, juices, or nonalcoholic punch for those who don't drink and for guests under twenty-one, the legal drinking age in most states. But to make the underaged feel more grown up, you might want to have a "virgin" frozen drink bar. Guests who do not care to drink alcohol or teens who want to give the impression they could order piña coladas, margaritas, or whatever else the bartender concocts can have them made without alcohol.

If you plan to serve dinner after an elaborate choreography and presentation, make sure your guests have something to nibble on. It can be as simple as small bowls of salted nuts and mints, or a lavish table of hot and cold hors d'oeuvres, cheeses, breads, and fruit.

The Presentation

The presentation, that magic moment when la quinceañera is presented as a young woman to her guests, is the dramatic high point of the evening. At Cuban and Puerto Rican celebrations, the presentation often comes at the beginning of the evening, when la quinceañera arrives at the party. Many times Mexican-American quinceñeras have dinner with their guests and are presented after dinner but before the dance. Details on the presentation and on the choreography that accompanies it are found in chapter 7.

The toast, thank-yous from la quinceañera and her parents, cutting the cake, and singing happy birthday can all be included in the presentation section of your reception. You can use them to punctuate and pace the reception and segue from one part to the next, in whatever order seems right for you.

The Toast

The toast, known as the *brindis,* is usually done after the presentation to congratulate the quinceañera on her passage to the next stage of her life. It is usually made by the announcer or master of ceremonies or a family member you want to have a special role: a godfather, a brother or sister, or a grandparent. Celia Hernandez was toasted with pink champagne that flowed from a silver fountain on the cake table. If you do not want the court to drink champagne, nonalcoholic cider or grape juice can serve as a substitute.

Sometimes, to cut costs, champagne will be served only to the parents of the court, the padrinos, and the immediate family. They will toast the quinceañera, rather than having everyone join in. Sometimes reception sites charge extra to have the waiters pour the champagne. Ana Maria Valenzuela wanted all the guests to join in a toast to her daughter, Laura. She had the banquet manager put a bottle of champagne on each table. When the time for the toast arrived, "we asked everybody to open the bottles, serve themselves, and stand up. They all did it, as a family type thing," Valenzuela said.

SAMPLE TOASTS

José Luis Ovalle's Toast to Laura Valenzuela

Felicidades en el futuro de esa bella joven, ejemplo para muchos de nuestros familias, y felicitemos también a sus padres, y a sus amigos y a toda la gente que a la bendición llegar a esta bella dama. Esperemos que tu juventud ser tan florida como ha sido su niñez. Salud!

Congratulations! To the future of this beautiful young person, who is an example to many of our families. We also congratulate her parents, her friends, and everyone who wishes blessings on this beautiful lady. We hope that your youth will be as flowery as your childhood has been. To your health!

A Toast from a Father to a Daughter

It hardly seems as though fifteen years have passed since your mother and I watched you take your first steps in our house, under our watchful eye. Now you are a young lady, about to take your first steps in the adult world. Everyone in the family has seen grace and intelligence, kindness and humor grow in you, to accompany you through life. We are all so very proud of you, no one more than your mother and I. May you always be blessed with life's sweetness, the way you have brought sweetness to our lives. *Salud!*

Thanks All Around

Giving thanks is an underlying theme in all quinceañera celebrations. Parents often throw the parties not just to mark the next phase of their daughter's life, but to show their appreciation for her. At some point during the reception, she thanks them in return.

Celia Hernandez's Thank-You to Her Parents

"You're wonderful parents. At this time, I wish to thank you for everything you have done for me, for being the best parents a girl could ask for. I love you both."

Ileana Perez's Message to Her Daughter, Teresita

"I'm so happy to have a daughter like you. You are the pride of my life. I pray to God, your guardian angel, and your grandfather, Pablo, that they guide you through your life and make all your dreams come true. The passing years won't matter, you'll always be my dear daughter. I love you."

Oscar Perez's Words to His Daughter, Teresita

"The dream of every woman who has children is to give a man a child like you. You are the best daughter in all the world. God blessed me the day he gave you to me. I ask God to bless you and be with you throughout your life. Your loving father."

Nadia Ali of Bay Shore, New York, thanked all the special people who brought the light of love into her life with a candle-lighting ceremony. Because she celebrated her passage from childhood as a Sweet Sixteen, she presented the sixteen most important people in her life with pink tapers decorated with lace and flowers on a Styrofoam base. To each one, she gave a short thank-you highlighting the reason why that person is special to her: her mother, for being her "best friend"; her stepfather, for teaching her how to drive; her "Titi Marilyn, for teaching me to listen and avoid nothing, and for making all that food out there"; her friends Phil and Linda Ramos, "for helping me with my party, and taking me on that skiing trip and showing me how to ski." The candles became souvenirs for the special people in her life.

Seating for the Dinner

Depending on your cultural and family tradition, the quinceañera may sit at a head table with her family or with her chambelán de honor and her court, her padrinos, or any combination of these.

Quinceañera and her family or padrinos: Quinceañera sits at the center. Going to the right to the end of the table: her mother, her youngest sibling, the next youngest sibling or maternal grandfather, maternal grandmother, any maternal aunts or uncles sitting next to their respective husbands or wives. On her left is her father. Next to him is her next youngest sibling or paternal grandmother, paternal grandfather, any paternal aunts and their husbands or uncles and their respective wives. Instead of the aunts and uncles, the most important padrinos may sit at the head table. The court sits with their families at tables bordering the dance floor.

Quinceañera and her court: The quinceañera sits at the center. To her left sits her chambelán de honor, then a dama, chambelán, and so forth. Next to the quinceañera on her right sits her dama de honor, if she has one. To the dama's right is her chambelán, then another dama, and so forth to the end of the table. If there is no dama de honor, another chambelán may sit there, with his dama to his right, another chambelán, and so forth.

Or the girls may sit to the quinceañera's right and the boys to her left, with her honor escort next to her. Her family sits at a table near the head table and near the chambelán de honor's family table.

Ask the site manager to arrange the tables so that everyone can see the dance floor, where the choreography and presentation will take place. At a less formal party, you may want everyone to sit at whatever guest table they please and with whomever else they choose. But for a more formal party, to keep things a bit more organized, you may want to decide not only who will sit at what tables but also where at the table they will sit. Designating seating arrangements can also help control any friction that exists between family members by placing them on opposite sides of the room. In your notebook of dreams, include a sketch of the room and the way you would like to see the tables set up. Number each table and keep a list of who should sit at each table. Then when it comes time to make up the place cards, which you will have arranged at the table in the entry-way, all you will have to do is write the name and table number on the card.

The Cake

A quinceañera is not complete without a cake, whether you call it *el pastel* or *el bizcocho.* Some of them are not only culinary feats, but engineering achievements to rival the rail-road tunnel beneath Mount Meiggs in Peru.

"It has to be a fancy cake," said Norma Garcia, who brought a picture of the cake she wanted from Puerto Rico and had someone make it in New York, where her daughter celebrated her quinceañera. "One of those with the bridges and the water, and many levels."

The most elaborate cakes are made up of several decorated layers that sit atop columns and connect to the main cake by bridges. Figurines representing the court of honor stand on the bridges, which span a fountain bubbling with colored water. Fresh flowers decorate the cake, and on the top, a quinceañera may stand in front of a lace fan. The whole thing can cost several thousand dollars if it is made by a commercial baker. You can often find people in the neighborhood who make the elaborate cakes in their homes for a fraction of what it would cost to have them made commercially.

Many people buy their cakes, for instance, from people like Rosario García, known around Washington Heights as Rosario *la Bizcochera.* García has made cakes in her apartment for nine years, and can make them as simple or as elaborate as you want. Her fee, which runs from $25 for a simple cake for fifteen people to $1,100 for an elaborate multitiered cake, includes delivery and set-up.

The quinceañera cake is traditionally a yellow cake with a fruit filling, but they vary from culture to culture. Dominicans pride themselves on rich, sweet cakes, while Puerto Ricans prefer their cakes lighter. Ask the baker for a sample, to make sure it's the cake you want.

Friends, family, and the party professionals you are working with are the best sources for recommendations on bakers. And do not overlook the grocery store. If it has a bakery section, chances are the bakers can produce the cake you are looking for—whether it's a simple sheet cake with dolls dressed to represent the quinceañera and her court or an elaborate multitiered extravaganza with a fountain, bridges, and a fancy topper.

Because the cake is an important element of the celebration, start working with the baker at least two to three months before the celebration. Be clear about the kind of cake you want, the number of people it will serve, and when and where it will be delivered and set up. Find out and arrange to have on hand what the baker will need—extension cords for the fountain, a table of a certain size, and so on.

If you are going to pick the cake up, make it part of the list of things to do the day of the party. At nine o'clock, when Fanny Padilla's celebration was in full swing, a little girl walked up to Fanny's mother, María Lourdes García de Padilla. " 'Where's the cake?' the girl asked me," Mrs. Padilla recalled. "Then I remembered I forgot to pick it up." Fortunately someone from the bakery was at the party, and the Padillas were able to get him to open the shop and get the cake!

This is, after all, a birthday party, and what birthday party would be complete without a rousing chorus of "Happy Birthday"? Most frequently, la quinceañera is serenaded with a chorus in English followed by a chorus in Spanish. A good time to break into the song is after the toast. If mariachis are playing at the reception, the singing of happy birthday may be put off until they arrive.

The Last Doll

Dolls are a frequent symbol at quinceañera receptions, especially at Dominican, Puerto Rican, and Mexican parties. They often decorate the cake, and serve as thank-you favors for the girls in the court of honor. A doll dressed identically to the quinceañera, right down to the color and style of her hair and the crown on her head, is made as a decoration and keepsake for this special day. Often the capias, the commemorative ribbon favors so popular at these events, are pinned to the skirt of the quinceañera doll. In Chicago, a baby doll is presented to the quinceañera by her father, symbolizing the last doll she will receive in her childhood.

The quinceañera doll symbolizes the perfection of youth, the moment when a girl leaves her childhood and becomes a young lady. She is forever captured as she was that day—her hairstyle, her dress, her crown. It represents the ideal—her fantasy, her fairy tale come true.

At Dominican and Puerto Rican celebrations, the quinceañera often walks around with her escort or another member of her court of honor, who carries the quinceañera doll laden with capias. They move from table to table, the quinceañera greeting each guest and pinning a capia on them to thank them for coming. The quinceañera doll may be used as a decoration at the entryway table or to designate the dinner table where the quinceañera herself will sit. The capias may be in a decorated basket, rather than on the doll's skirt.

The doll is often presented toward the end of the dance, usually by the girl's father or both parents. Whether the quinceañera doll or a baby doll is presented as the last doll, it serves as a reminder of the night the girl crossed from childhood toward womanhood, a reminder of what she will be leaving behind. (For more information on the last doll, see chapter 12.)

FACING PAGE: *Twins Jessica and Jarlyn Romero share highlights of their celebration during the dinner at their party.*
—© 1995 *Newsday*

Chapter Five

Padrinos y Madrinas:
The Mexican American Tradition of Sponsors

> The padrinos participate largely because of the nature of their relationship, not out of economic necessity. It's a statement about trust or *confianza* between relatives or compadres.
>
> —*Ruth Horowitz*

Felicia Aguirre was covering new ground among her Mexican American family in San Antonio, Texas. No one on her mother's side—eleven sisters and sisters-in-law in all—or among her father's people had ever had a quinceañera before. So when Felicia's mother, Rita, announced Felicia was going to make her debut, everyone was very excited. Many of them wanted to help. Rita Aguirre's first step in planning was to line up the sponsors, the padrinos and madrinas—the extended family members she hoped she could count on for a contribution to the celebration.

Most Latino families, regardless of their cultural background, pull together to make a quinceañera happen. The aunts and cousins will get together with the quinceañera and her mother to make the decorations, or an uncle will recommend a band or disc jockey.

FACING PAGE: *A wave of emotion catches Lori Hernandez when her* padrinos *present their gifts to the Reverend Jim O'commor for his blessing during Lori's mass of thanksgiving at Our Lady of Guadalupe Roman Catholic Church in Lubbock, Texas.* —Sharon M. Steinman

The quinceañera and her parents, of course, know who made what possible as gifts to the birthday girl.

But among Mexican Americans, the help of a girl's godparents, relatives, and family friends is often solicited from the beginning. The head of the family asks people to be padrinos, or sponsors.

Just as the quinceañera marks a girl's transition from childhood to young adulthood, it also marks the reinforcement of the relationship between her parents and the sponsors. In recognition of their generosity, the sponsors' names and the items they made possible are printed in the invitations. Those who contributed the five gifts—the prayer book and rosary, the crown, the medal, the bracelet, and the earrings—sometimes also precede the court of honor in the processional into the church service and at the reception. The padrinos and their families are invited to the celebration, and often are permitted to invite another couple, if not that couple's family, to the quinceañera as well. They become the community that not only honors the quinceañera as she passes from her childhood, but to which she is presented as a young woman.

Most often, as soon as you announce that you are planning a celebration, your family will volunteer, either to buy things directly or to pitch in additional funds for your needs. Once the Leal family, also of San Antonio, Texas, announced they were going to throw a quinceañera for their youngest daughter, Marie, members of the extended family volunteered information on who could do what. A cousin who was part of a band gave them a deep discount on their fee. An aunt's mother-in-law created the dress. Marie's father got a deal on the officers' club at Kelly Air Force Base in San Antonio, where he was stationed while in the military and then worked as a civilian.

Many of our indigenous cultures include ritual kinship—the social ties that elevate friendship to symbolic inclusion in the family or strengthen the bond between two families through participation in the ceremonies that mark life's milestones. Reciprocity, the idea of returning social favors, was also an important element among our indigenous ancestors. It is likely that the Catholic Church drew upon those customs when they developed *padrinazgo*, godparenthood or sponsorship.

Padrinazgo carried sacred as well as financial responsibilities and duties toward the child. People are invited to be padrinos for baptisms, confirmations, and weddings as well as quinceañeras, although baptismal padrinos are the most important. So close is the bond between the godparents and the birth parents that they refer to each other as *compadre*, or coparent. Indeed, the Catholic Church considered the relationship so strong that it prohibited marriage between padrinos and their *ahijados*, godparents and their godchildren, or even between their godchildren and their biological children.

"Some of the worldly-wise folk invite persons outside of their own social class to act as godparents because they can afford costlier gifts," wrote Frances Toor in *A Treasury of Mexican Folkways.* "Such invitations are refused only for very good reasons, and as long as the relationship lasts there is an exchange of gifts, favors, and hospitality."

Choosing the Sponsors

Toor was writing about traditional Mexican custom. Here, padrinazgo affirms an established relationship, rather than develops a new one. Hank Roa, the executive director of the Mexican Folkloric Dance Company of Chicago, said that total strangers have asked him to sponsor their daughters' quinceañeras.

"I said no," Roa recalled. "The parents should really think about how they're going to pay for the party. The further away you get from the border and into the second generation, the more people get away from sponsors."

The immediate family, the extended family, godparents, the parents of any godchildren you have, and anyone your family has sponsored for a baptism, a quinceañera, or a wedding are all potential contributors to your celebration. For the Martinezes of Chicago, their daughter's quinceañera was a chance to reap all the goodwill and help they had sown with others when they were asked to be padrinos. "We did have a budget and my husband went to his friends, all the friends he had helped before, for weddings and all that," said Susana Martinez. Sponsorship not only assures you of help in the present, but also obligates you and the quinceañera to help the sponsors when their daughters come of age.

Your budget will determine how many sponsors you need and how much you ask each one to contribute. Do not forget that they have families and bills to pay themselves. The contribution you request should be reasonable, generally between $50 and

❧ ❧ *When You Wish upon a Padrino* ❧ ❧

Make a list of the things you want in your quinceañera so when a sponsor asks you what you need, you will know. Here are some of the things that you may want sponsored:

bouquet for the Virgin Mary, if there is
   going to be a Catholic mass
bracelet
cake
cake knife and server
capia doll
capias
choreographer
church service souvenirs or cards
church, which may but does not have to
   include the decorations and the music
crown
cushions for the quinceañera to kneel
   on at the altar
dinner
drinks
earrings
invitations
last doll

limousine
mariachi at the church, reception, or both
medal
music
photography
prayer book or Bible and rosary
quinceañera's bouquet
quinceañera's dress
reception site
ring
ceramic souvenirs to be given to the guests
   at the reception
table decorations
toasting glasses for the court and sponsors
toasting glasses for the quinceañera and
   her escort
videography
watch

$100. Often sponsors will offer more. If all your padrinos come through, they may cover between 20 and 50 percent of the cost of the quinceañera. The fail-safe method, however, is to be prepared to pay for all the expenses yourself. Then when sponsors pay for an element or contribute money for the celebration, you can use the extra money to add a detail you otherwise would have done without. Be sure to keep a cash reserve of 20 percent of the total cost of the celebration to cover expenses that may arise as a result of unforeseen circumstances.

Apart from their financial assistance, the padrinos can also serve as a tremendous planning resource, sort of a committee to help the family find the elements they want included in the celebration. "Every aspect of the ceremony has to be thought out," said Ramiro Burr, a music journalist. "That's why you need a committee to help you. Someone's got to bring in the appropriate knickknacks. Someone's got to pay for the appropriate drinks. Someone's got to pay for the entertainment. Someone will pay for the food and the catering. Someone's got to take care of the limousine. Every aspect needs someone who's going to participate and know what he's doing."

In your notebook of dreams, make a list of all the people you think might be willing to be sponsors for the celebration—immediate and extended family; friends; people you have sponsored for a social occasion. Be sure to write down their telephone numbers and any areas of expertise or special connections they may have.

Make a separate list of items available for sponsorship. When people ask what you need help with, you will be ready to tell them.

Inviting Sponsorship

Begin with the people you are closest to. They are the ones most likely to help. The sooner you invite the sponsors to participate, the more time you will give them to come up with the money to pay for their contribution. You might want to ask them during a telephone conversation announcing your plans shortly after you have decided to have a quinceañera celebration. Often family members and close friends will ask you what they can do to help before you bring up sponsorship. Keep track of what they have committed to help with, whether it's a cash contribution or a specific item. When you receive their contribution, note that in your notebook as well.

Some of your closest family may volunteer to pay for big-ticket items. Felicia Aguirre's older brother, Larry, and his best friend paid several thousand dollars toward her celebration. They took care of the hall and the decorations, which included the flowers, the decoration of the church, the hall, and all the sponsors' ribbons. Aguirre said that once she gave her son the date on which the party was to be held, he took care of everything as his gift to his younger sister. Aguirre said she never knew what they

Michael Eid's
Advice for Buying Jewelry

Michael Eid, a jeweler in Fort Lauderdale, Florida, who stocks items to commemorate a fifteenth birthday, has advice for people who are looking for jewelry.

1. Ask questions. Is the ring or medal you are buying made of gold? Or is it base metal or gold plate? The purity of gold is measured in karats with 24-karat gold being pure, 12-karat gold composed of half that amount. Ask the jeweler what the karat weight of the piece you are interested in buying is. It should be stamped on the piece. If you do not ask, the jeweler does not have to tell you.

2. Know your jeweler. Is he or she reputable? Have they been in business for a number of years? Or are they less established?

3. Ask for a discount. It could save you between two and five percent off the price of the piece.

paid for the elements they sponsored.

More often, especially for the big-ticket items, such as the banquet hall, the band, the photography or videography, or even the cake, sponsors will give a cash contribution. Those contributions are then pooled to take care of each item. The Leals chose what they wanted—the band, for example—and then members of the extended family pitched in to pay for it.

The five gifts that are blessed in church—the ring or bracelet, the medal or cross and necklace, the crown, the prayer book or Bible and rosary, and earrings—and sometimes presented there are most often given by close family members. The symbolism of the gifts is explained on pages 38–39. Sometimes, instead of a bracelet or a ring, the quinceañera will receive a watch, representing the passage of time and the future that lies ahead. Instead of earrings, she may receive flowers, denoting the newness of her commitment and responsibility to the community.

Generally the sponsors who pay for the smaller items—such as the capias, the ribbon favors each guest gets at the reception, the cake knife and server—select those items themselves. They are, after all, gifts to the quinceañera. You need to keep the sponsor informed of your plans—theme, color scheme, the church, the reception site—and any other details that will help them in choosing their item.

For the Sponsors

In Mexico, when someone is invited to be a padrino, death, either yours or a member of your immediate family, is almost the only acceptable excuse to decline. Yet because quinceañeras are not nearly as expensive to have there as they are in the United States, the parents often foot the entire bill themselves. There the padrinos serve a more spiritual role, closer to godparents. Their expenditure is time and caring, rather than money.

But in the United States, sometimes the request comes at the wrong time, when money is tight or unexpected expenses arise. While the sponsors' contributions in cash or kind are welcome, they are not the only way one can make the effort to create a special day. There are many ways to help, from making some of the food to decorating the hall, making centerpieces for the tables at the reception, or even helping the damas in the court with their hair on the day of the celebration. Be honest with yourself and with the person organizing the quinceañera about what role you can take on, whether financial or otherwise.

Although the final selection of whatever item you are sponsoring is up to you, working closely with the quinceañera and her mother will help make your decision easier. Keep them abreast of what you are considering, just to make sure your choice fits in with the "dream scheme." Let them know when you have made the final selection and what arrangements you have made to get your contribution where it needs to be on time. That way the organizers will have one less detail to keep track of.

Sometimes the Unexpected Happens

Sponsors are can be a tremendous economic help, and their intentions are always the best. Sometimes, however, unforeseen events arise and they are unable to keep their promises. The closer your relationship with your sponsor, the more willing, generous, and up-front with you they are likely to be if they cannot honor their commitment. Many times, when someone asks us for a favor, we hate to say no. This is why it's so important to have a well-established relationship with whomever you ask to be a sponsor.

The guests at a quinceañera in Chicago had eaten their dinner and the mariachis had finished playing. The low rumble of conversation filled the room as everyone waited for the band to arrive so the dance could start. Finally the quinceañera went to her father, who called the band's manager to find out where they were.

Yes, the band manager told the father, a man with the padrino's name had contacted them a number of months ago about playing that night. Yes, they said, they had had it free at the time. The manager said he quoted a price, but the man never returned to put down a deposit, and another job had come in. They weren't coming.

Most times the excitement of planning the quinceañera celebration keeps the telephone ringing between the homes of the sponsors and the organizers, with details of their latest finds, the latest decisions and developments. If you are relying on padrinos to finance a sizable portion of the celebration, take stock of where things stand two to three months before the party, about the time you are ready to finalize the guest list. You may decide to revise your plans. José Luis Ovalle, the artistic director of the Mexican Folkloric Dance Company of Chicago who also choreographs quinceañera waltzes, had a cousin who threw a quince años party for his daughter. They picked a date, picked out a dress for the quinceañera, chose the color of the dresses for the damas in the court, and ordered tuxedos for the chambelanes. They shopped around for the best prices. Finally, three months before the party, they sat down, balanced the budget, and revised their final plans. They cut back on the number of people they would invite. The full court of fourteen couples was reduced to four chambelanes, the quinceañera's escort, and the quinceañera herself. The sponsors were unable to give as much money as the quinceañera's family had hoped for.

There Aren't Enough Thanks . . .

They are the producers of your celebration, the family and friends who have contributed money or time or expertise. They are nearly as proud of you as your parents.

And for their efforts, they must be thanked. But a simple thank-you is far from enough. They are *your* guests of honor and as such are recognized in several different ways.

- On the invitations. If you have kept good notes in your notebook of dreams, this will be a snap. Every item that was sponsored is listed with the name of the person or couple who bought it. The list is generally printed on tissue in one of the theme colors and inserted into the invitations given to the guests.
- With a corsage or boutonniere. These do not have to be of fresh flowers, although they can be. Many times, they are made of ribbon or sculpted from *migajón de pan*, the malleable dough that looks like porcelain when dry.
- At the church. Often the prime padrinos, the ones who have bought the gifts and have paid for the church and the church decorations and the music played during the service, are included in the processional. The prime padrinos sit in the very front rows of the church, with the parents and the court of honor. The other padrinos sit in the rows just behind them. Depending on the number of padrinos you have, they may all walk in the processional, if the church allows it.
- At the reception. Depending on how many there are, the padrinos may sit at the head table. Usually, however, there are so many that the quinceañera's immediate family, her grandparents, and any aunts and uncles, all of whom are usually padrinos, sit at the head table. The rest of the padrinos sit with their families at tables closest to the dance floor. They are always at the front, just behind the quinceañera, if *la marcha* is done. *La marcha* is traditionally done in the western states, such as Colorado and Texas. The quinceañera and her parents lead the court of honor, the padrinos, and the guests in figures around the tables and end in the middle of the dance floor. At the place where each padrino sits, there is a special favor made especially for them. They are included in the thank-you the quinceañera reads at the reception. If there are many of them, they do not all have to be named. A line thanking "all my padrinos for their generosity" is fine.
- With thank-you notes. They should be the first thank-you notes the quinceañera writes. Without their help, the fairy princess would have had a hard time attending the ball.

Chapter Six

The Court of Honor

> The kids in the court are thinking about the fun they're going to have, but their parents have a completely different perspective. The only thing the parents are thinking is how much is this going to cost me?
>
> —*Mariano Arceo, a popular chambelán*

Jackie Delao's honor court stepped out of cars in front of the First Congregational Church in Danbury, Connecticut, one snowy March day, but they looked as if they had stepped off the pages of a fashion magazine. The girls wore elegant dark green sheath dresses with matching pumps and carried small bouquets of pink-edged roses. The boys sported black tuxedos over dark green brocade vests. Their white-gloved hands carried black canes. Jackie, looking like Cinderella in her gold and white brocade gown, stood radiant among them. At the reception later that evening, they would perform three dances that they had practiced every week for three months to Jackie's favorite songs.

What is a princess without an honor court to attend her?

The court of honor may trace its origins to the palace of the Duchess of Alba in eighteenth-century Spain, where the duchess herself is credited by some with starting the quinceañera custom. The duchess would invite girls on the cusp of womanhood to the palace, where she would dress them and make them up as adults for the first time. Similarly, although a century later, the Empress Carlota of Mexico invited the daughters

FACING PAGE: *Isabel Prida's court of honor salutes her in the finale of their choreography at her quinces in Miami.*
—Enrique Muñoz Studio.

of the members of her court to be presented as young ladies eligible for marriage. In both cases, there would be a party, with a feast and the dancing of intricate figures, as was the custom of the time, a custom that is carried over to the quinceañera celebration today.

Today the boys and girls who stand in the court of honor are the quinceañera's contemporaries, the people to whom she feels closest, the people from whom she draws her strength, the people who are her community—her sisters and brothers, her cousins and closest friends. They mean so much to the quinceañera that to be in the spotlight without them is unthinkable.

Being in a court is fun, pure and simple. It gives the teens a chance to dress up in gowns and tuxedos, wear makeup, and put on heels. They get to act like grown-ups. But being in a court is more than putting on fancy clothes and going to an elegant party. It takes loyalty, commitment, dedication, and self-respect to get through the months of practice and preparation. Those who choose to participate are part of something priceless—creating a beautiful birthday celebration for someone special.

The court of honor lends charm to a quinceañera. Careful planning and careful selection of the people you ask to stand in your court will make the occasion a memorable one. Begin by deciding how you want your court composed. You may want any combination of these participants:

- The chambelán de honor, or honor escort, is the quinceañera's date for the evening.
- The dama de honor, or maid of honor, is a largely ceremonial role given to the girl to whom the quinceañera feels closest. She may be asked to do a reading at the church service or to pin the ribbon favors known as capias on the guests. She may be a best friend, a sister, or a cousin.
- The damas and chambelanes are the quinceañera's contemporaries who make up the bulk of the court.
- The flower girl is generally between six and ten years old. Her sole job is to strew flower petals before the quinceañera's feet.
- The prince and princess are generally younger family members who are given a special role. The princess's role, generally, is to strew the quinceañera's path with flower petals if there is no flower girl. The prince generally escorts the princess. Sometimes

Quinceañeras traditionally had a court of all girls, like Maria Antonia Reyes did at her celebration in San Antonio, Texas, in 1956. —Courtesy of the Reyes family

the prince and princess carry the crown and shoes in Mexican, Puerto Rican, and Central American celebrations. You can have as many princes and princesses as you have little cousins, generally between five and eight years old.

- The good luck girl, also known as the symbol of innocence, is a tiny child, usually between two and four years old, dressed identically to the quinceañera, right down to the crown. She represents the quinceañera as a little girl, and is most often seen at Central American, Dominican, and Puerto Rican quinceañera celebrations.

What Kind of Court Do I Want?

The court you choose is up to you, depending on how elaborate a celebration you plan, how many people you want to honor with this very special invitation, and the kind of presentation you want to have at your party. There are many variations on the court:

- The full court or classic court features fourteen boys and fourteen girls, each couple representing one year of life. The quinceañera and the honor escort make fifteen.

- The half court features seven girls and seven boys, each person represents a year in the quinceañera's life.

- An all-girl court ideally has fourteen girls. Millie Negrón had this court for her celebration in Chicago. The girls were between the ages of one and fourteen, each one literally representing a year of her life. As her mother, Enit, announced the name of each girl, she read a list of achievements Millie had accomplished at that age. Finally, the sum of all her fifteen years, Millie herself entered the hall, to the applause of her family and friends. For families that believe the quinceañera celebration is supposed to be the girl's first social contact with boys, this would be an appropriate court. At Celia Hernandez's quinceañera, she had eight girls in her court. At the reception, each girl made her entrance on her own father's arm.

- An all-boy court of between four and fourteen boys. Some people feel an all-boy court puts more focus on the quinceañera herself.

- A simple court generally has three variations: an honor escort or a dama de honor, or the quinceañera escorted by her parents, or just her father.

Whether the court includes just your contemporaries or the extended family as well is determined by your cultural background. Among Cubans and some Puerto Ricans, the court is generally considered to be only the damas and chambelanes. Among Mexican Americans and other Puerto Ricans, the court includes not only the damas and chambe-

❧ ❧ *What Are They Called?* ❧ ❧

The quinceañera celebration is common to all Latino cultures. But just as the Spanish spoken can be markedly different from country to country, so are the words for the boys who participate in the court. Among the Mexicans and Cubans, a boy in a court is a *chambelán,* a chamberlain. But in Puerto Rico, he is an *escorte,* an escort. In the Dominican Republic, he may be called a *galán,* a courtier. But a girl is always a *dama,* a lady.

lanes but also a flower girl and a prince and princess. Mexican Americans also sometimes include the padrinos of the gifts (see chapter 5) and the grandparents as well. The symbol of innocence is popular among Puerto Ricans, Dominicans, and Central Americans.

How large you want your court to be is for you to decide. What is important is to craft a celebration that reflects you and your family, your traditions and your heritage.

Selecting Your Court of Honor

The court of honor is one of the most enchanting traditions of the quinceañera celebration. It intensifies the focus of the celebration on youth, on the transition from childhood to adulthood. Just as the planning and preparation for the celebration helps the quinceañera herself to mature, the people she chooses to be her court of honor accompany her in this rite of passage. There is plenty of fun along the way: shopping for dresses, fittings, learning new dances, trying new food. But if 90 percent of life is just showing up, it's especially true for a quinceañera's court of honor. This is what you will be asking them to do for the next three months or so:

- Come to the choreography rehearsals every week for as long as three months, depending on how complex the presentation and waltz are. Ideally in between rehearsals, they should practice what they learned the week before.
- Spend between $50 and $300 on what they will wear and how they will look on the day of the party.
- Arrive promptly for rehearsals, fittings, and any religious preparation the church may require in preparation for a service.
- Perhaps read one of the Scripture passages during the church service, if you are having one.

The most important attributes the members of the court can have are commitment and a good attitude. You will want to choose people who will back you up all the way, who are willing to learn the dance steps you or the choreographer create. Choosing people who just do not care about making their best effort robs the fun from the rehearsals and ultimately from the celebration itself. "It's hard picking a court when you have to get thirty kids, but try to pick people who want to learn at the practices," said Rosendo Ramon, a choreographer in Miami who specializes in quinces. "I don't mind teaching thirty kids who don't know anything about dancing, as much as having thirty kids in a rehearsal who know how to dance but don't care about the quinces."

Often people are in demand to stand in courts of honor, so extend your invitation early enough to avoid potential scheduling conflicts and to allow them to save the money for their dresses and tuxedos. If the worst happens and someone has to drop out, there is time to replace them or adjust the choreography if they tell you soon enough.

Finding girls to be in a court is usually not a problem, but finding their escorts sometimes can be. Girls mature more quickly than boys, and the idea of participating in a formal party is more appealing to girls than to boys in their early teens. Often the quinceañera picks her male family or friends. Sometimes the damas themselves are asked to pick their own escorts, who are often their boyfriends. Other times the quinceañera turns to the honor escort to find escorts for the girls from among his friends. Often that's the best solution. Keep in mind that having boys and girls who are dating each other participate in a court can create problems if they break up before the celebration.

Who should and should not be in the court of honor can be a major point of contention between the quinceañera and her parents. Often the quinceañera wants her friends from school to be in her court. Her parents, however, may not know them, let alone their families. Parents generally prefer to have family members or the children of family friends participate in the court.

Maria Magaña and her mother, Leticia, agree that she should have all boys in her court and only one dama de honor. Six months before her debut, they had not agreed on how many (Maria wanted fourteen, her mother only seven) or who should be in her court.

"She wants them all to be tall and handsome," said Leticia Magaña. "The truth is, I want her to have people from the family or someone we know. If she invites someone and they're part of a gang, there could be problems at the party. That's why I don't want her to invite anyone other than her cousins and people we know."

Reaching out to the extended family to participate in the court of honor strengthens family ties and can open a whole new social world to the quinceañera. Marisela Martinez got to know her brother-in-law's family through her celebration. Her sister, Julie, turned to them when they were looking for people to stand in Marisela's honor court. A lot of her brother-in-law's cousins were only too happy to participate. In the end, the only person to drop out was one of Marisela's school friends. The family all stood by her.

Dollars and Sense

If the quinceañera makes a fantasy reality, the first step is to learn what is realistic. One girl and half her court came into Elegant Touch, Paulette Peace's bridal and formal-wear shop on Long Island, New York, to look for dresses. The ones they fell in love with were $350, said Peggy Peace, who does much of the sewing in her daughter's shop. When one of the parents came to see the dress the next day, they took one look at the price tag and issued a pocketbook veto.

Sometimes the cost of being in the court contributes to someone's decision to drop out. Teens in a court often rely on their parents for the money to pay for their expenses, because most of them are too young to hold jobs. As you select what the court will wear, try to keep costs to a minimum or to stretch payment out over several months to give them time to raise the money. A simple dress for the damas can be just as elegant as

❧ ❧ *Professional Chambelanes?* ❧ ❧

You have begged your family and friends and their family and friends for weeks, and you are still short escorts. What to do? Hire professional chambelanes. Sometimes they are budding quinces choreographers in their own right. Sometimes they are dancers in local folkloric companies. For a fee plus expenses, they can fill in the gap. You can find them by word of mouth, through dressmakers who specialize in quinceañera dresses and decorations, formal-wear rental shops, or reception sites that have held quinceañera celebrations. Unfortunately, demand has not created a similar career path for damas.

one with a lot of ruffles and beadwork, and will be easier on your budget. Shopping around for the best deal on fifteen tuxedos will save money for the escorts. Having your friends at the house who can do the girls' hair and makeup could save them money at the hairdresser.

If you know the parents of the teens who will be in the court, you may have a better idea of what is affordable and what is not. Bear in mind, however, that many times the quinceañera's friends want to participate because everyone else from their group is. No one likes to say he or she cannot afford to be in a court. If a member of the court is several weeks late paying a deposit for a dress or a tuxedo, have a talk with him or her. If the problem is money, you may want to pay for their expenses rather than risk having that person drop out and scrambling to find a replacement.

If You Are Asked to Be in a Court

The quinceañera thinks the world of you and wants you to be close to her on one of the most important days of her life. Being asked to be in a court is both an honor and a privilege. If you accept the quinceañera's invitation, you are promising her you will be reliable and dedicated to making the celebration a success. While learning new dances, meeting new friends, wearing nice clothes to a fancy party are all part of the fun of being in a court, there are also challenges to meet along the way.

- **The expense.** Being in a court of honor can be expensive. The quinceañera will ask you to be in the court as soon as possible and will no doubt tell you within a few weeks what you can expect to pay for whatever you will be wearing. Talk with your parents and see how much of the expense they are able to cover. Offer to do odd jobs around the house, like babysit for a younger brother or sister or clean the basement or garage, in addition to any responsibilities you may have as a way to earn extra cash. Do you think you can come up with the money?
- **The time commitment.** Dancing in the choreography is your big moment in the spotlight. Especially at Cuban quinces, the production may be elaborate, with as many as a

dozen dances to learn. You may be asked to come to rehearsal once a week for up to twelve weeks. In addition, there will be fittings for the dresses or tuxedos and sometimes a weekend retreat at the church, if the quinceañera is going to have a service. Will you have the time to be where you are needed ?

♦ **The social aspect.** A dama may be asked to bring her own escort. While your first inclination is to bring your boyfriend, that may not be the wisest choice. If you break up before the party, can you stand to see him at rehearsal? Will you be able to dance with him? You may want to consider bringing a cousin or a brother instead. If you do not know anyone who might want to stand with you, can the quinceañera or her honor escort find someone for you?

Whether you are a dama or a chambelán, if your boyfriend or girlfriend is not in the court and you will be with another person that night, is that going to be a problem for you? You may be paired with someone you find very attractive and want to start seeing outside the rehearsals. Before you do, think of what may happen if you break up. You have both committed to being in the court. If either of you drops out because

What Does It Cost to Be in a Court?

FOR THE DAMAS

Dress	Makeup
Shoes	Manicure
Stockings	Headpiece
Any lingerie—	Sometimes the
bras, slips, or	bouquet, corsage,
crinolines that the	or wrist corsage, if
dress may need	not bought by
Jewelry	the escorts
Hair	

The total for a dama to participate in a court can range from $100 to several hundred dollars, depending on what part of the country the quinceañera is held in, what she'll be wearing, and the package that's negotiated with the dressmaker or bridal shop.

FOR THE CHAMBELANES

Tuxedo rental	Braces
Tie	Boutonniere
Cummerbund	Sometimes their
or vest	lady's bouquet,
Shirt	corsage, or wrist
Studs	corsage
Shoes	

The cost to participate in a court as a chambelán generally runs between $50 and $150, depending on the area of the country the quinceañera is being held in and the price the organizer was able to negotiate.

you do not want to see the other, it puts the quinceañera in a very difficult position of having to find a last-minute replacement for one or both of you. You owe it to the birthday girl, the rest of the court, and yourself to stay in, no matter how much you may want to drop out.

You may be paired with someone you find unattractive or dull. Bear in mind that the person you are paired with is not a reflection on you. That person was asked to be in the court because he or she is important to the quinceañera, just as you are. She knew she could count on him or her no matter what, which is why she invited you to be close to her, too.

If you have doubts about any of these areas that you think would prevent you from honoring your commitment to be in the court, you should probably decline. Tell the quinceañera how honored and flattered you are that she would invite you to play such an important part in her celebration, but that you are unable to accept her kind invitation. If you feel that you can help her in other ways, such as going with her to listen to bands or disc jockeys or making yourself available as a sounding board if she needs to talk, then offer to do so. If she asks you why you cannot be in the court, be honest but tactful with her. She and her mother may find a way for you to participate after all, if you really want to.

Older members of the court should set the example for the younger ones. Paulette Peace and her escort were nineteen when they stood in a celebration on Long Island, New York. "We knew some of the dances better than the sixteen-year-olds, so we helped them," Peace said. "We always went first, to get the other kids into it. The coordinator would show us how to do a couple of steps. So we started and everyone followed."

The quinceañera and her family appreciate the effort and expense you have gone through to be in the court, but courtesy is always appropriate. A thank-you for a ride to a rehearsal or a fitting and for the refreshments served at a practice is always welcome.

In Miami, the members of the court pool their resources together and get the quinceañera a gift. It can be money or jewelry, or something you know she has wanted. In other parts of the country, however, just participating in the court is considered enough of a gift. For the months of work and expenses, the families of the members of the court—or at least their parents—are usually invited, and they usually bring gifts.

For Damas Only

You are the quinceañera's counsel and her strength, her sympathetic ear and someone to make her laugh. How much or how little she asks you to do will depend on her. She may seek your opinion on the dresses, the colors, the band, or anything else she may have on her mind—which during the year before the party can be a lot.

The closer you are to the birthday girl, the more likely she will turn to you for support before the celebration. When Aina Gonzalez stood as a dama for her best friend, Valerie Bonilla, she helped pick the dresses and even went with Bonilla to audition bands. Bonilla also asked Gonzalez to do a reading at the mass.

When the specter of someone dropping out appears, the court often puts pressure on the wavering dama to stay in until the end. That happened in one of the quinceañeras that Aina Gonzalez stood in, when the quinceañera and her best friend, one of the damas, had a serious disagreement. "We had all been friends since middle school," said Gonzalez. "It was kind of shaky on the day of the debut."

If you hear someone is about to drop out of the court, talk with her to find out why. There may be something you can do to convince her to stay. She will feel better for honoring her commitment and the celebration will go on as planned without the quinceañera or her mother having to cope with replacing whoever dropped out.

For Chambelanes Only

Mariano Arceo has stood in five quinces in two years and was a favorite to be his cousin's chambelán de honor. His advice to guys who plan to stand in a quinceañera is simple: Do not play around and learn the steps to the choreographed dances.

Throughout the day and evening of the celebration, you and the girl you are escorting will have more fun if you're attentive to her, even though you both may be dating other people. Traditionally, by accepting to stand with a girl in a court of honor, you are expected to be pleasant company to her during your time together. That means picking her up, if other arrangements are not made, and making sure you both arrive where you are supposed to be promptly. You should dance at least the first and last dance with the young lady you are escorting, and get her food and drink throughout the evening or go with her to get it. Ask the quinceañera and each of the damas to dance at least once during the reception. The point is to mix and socialize with everyone.

THE CHAMBELÁN DE HONOR, OR HONOR ESCORT

His role is second only to the quinceañera herself and her parents. The chambelán de honor often escorts the quinceañera's mother into and the quinceañera herself out of any church service there may be. The honor escort is the quinceañera's main dance partner after she waltzes with her father at the reception. He is her prince charming for the evening. It is his job to be attentive to her and to make her look good whenever she is on his arm.

"You dance more if you're a chambelán, but your part's more important if you're the chambelán de honor," said Arceo, who is from Cicero, Illinois. "Everyone else looks up to you. You have to learn how to dance something different from the rest of the court, because you're dancing with the quinceañera."

In some families, only a brother or a cousin can be a chambelán de honor, because, theoretically, a girl is not old enough to know boys outside the family socially before she has been presented to the community as a young woman. Other times a quinceañera asks a member of the family to escort her because the bond between them is more enduring. Norma Garcia's daughter thought about asking her boyfriend to stand as her chambelán de honor, and then decided to ask both her brothers to fill the role. Her daughter's reasoning was "If I stop liking the boy, then I'm stuck with these pictures of someone I probably don't want to see again. These are my brothers and they'll always be my brothers," Norma Garcia said. Her friends and cousins made up the rest of the court. No one dropped out. Most of the time, however, the chambelán de honor is someone the quinceañera is dating or would like to date.

Marie Leal had already broken up with her boyfriend, but when her family started planning, he was the one she wanted at her side. "She was *cierta* she wanted to have him," said her oldest sister, Diana Leal Sandoval. "We were like 'Why? He may not even want to be there.' She asked him and he said he would stand in with her. She had him there. But that's the thing about the quinceañeras. They're hard sometimes to predict."

For the Parents

Whoever said life is in the details must have known something about quinceañeras. While the parents—most often the mother—are running around to find the best prices on everything from halls to table decorations, from dresses to souvenirs, they also have to keep an eye not only on the needs of the court, but who is in the court.

"I made sure for both their debuts that they chose real close friends and family," said Sarah Arevalo, Benita's mother, who had thrown a quinces for her older daughter two years earlier.

Keeping the court organized and on track can be one of the biggest challenges in creating a quinceañera celebration. Here are some tips:

1. Expect the unexpected, whether it's a member of the court dropping out at the last minute or several of them missing the church ceremony because they were stopped for a traffic ticket. Make a plan in advance just in case you need to conceal an unexpected absence.

2. Transportation is a hidden issue. If someone needs a ride to get to a fitting or rehearsal or to pick up a tuxedo, you may have to provide that ride. Make sure all your transportation details are worked out in advance.

3. It's not enough to know the teens in your daughter's court—get to know their parents as well. "When you tend to know the parents of the children that are in the debut, you're not going to have too many problems," said Rita Aguirre. "If you tend to see those parents at meetings and baseball games, they're more likely to follow through with their promises."

4. Teenagers are not as forthright as adults about what they need or what they can and

cannot do. They can be shy about saying whether they have a ride or can make a deposit on a tuxedo, or in regard to any of a hundred other issues that come up during a quinceañera. Make an effort to develop a relationship with each teen. Then they will be more likely to tell you if there is something they need help with.

5. In your planner or notebook, keep all the details related to the court: their names, addresses, and phone numbers; the dates of the fittings, where the fittings are held, who went, and when; who paid their deposits. If they do not pay the deposits or show up for fittings when they are supposed to, they may have second thoughts about participating.

6. Remember that you are dealing with children. They break up and then get back together. They have a new romantic interest every two or three months, if not weeks. You will be dealing with this for a year.

At the rehearsals, the choreographer is in charge, but it's up to you to provide refreshments and snacks. Peggy Peace said that everyone in her goddaughter's court had a blast because the parents turned each rehearsal into a small party.

A COURT NEWSLETTER

To keep the members of the court abreast of things they should know—like the name and address of the church and reception hall, where to buy their dresses and attire, what time they are supposed to be where, and how much everything costs—it's a good idea to make up a flyer or newsletter. It can be something simple written out by hand and copied, or a sophisticated sheet printed on colored paper that matches the theme, bordered with a motif and produced on a computer. The point is to give all the members of the court clear, detailed information consistently on paper. Keep extra newsletters in the section of your notebook you have designated for the court. If they forget or their parents ask a question covered in the newsletter, you can send them one. It also helps you keep track of what you told them and when.

A Promise Is Meant to Be Kept

Your plans are proceeding. The rehearsals are going well, everyone is learning their steps. And then the bomb falls—at the last minute someone drops out. Your stomach feels as though it's plunging to your feet.

There are as many reasons for dropping out as there are quinceañeras. One girl who had promised to stand in Marisela Martinez's court dropped out with less than a week to go because her mother wanted to bring more family than the Martinezes could accommodate. Ileana Perez scrambled and found not one but two replacements for people who dropped out, including the chambelán de honor. Two weeks after Teresita Perez had asked her boyfriend to stand with her as her chambelán de honor, they broke up and the boy decided he did not want to be in the court. Ileana Perez replaced him with her nephew. But then three weeks before the celebration, another chambelán dropped out. "His grades were very bad and his mom decided to punish him," Ileana Perez said. She called the choreographer with whom she had been working and asked him to replace the boy who dropped out. He did. And the choreography came out beautifully.

Lisa Alfaro of Chicago had originally planned on a full court of fourteen couples. Four months before her debut, she started rehearsals, every Sunday at her home. At first her friends were very enthusiastic and came to the rehearsals. But around the third practice, one of the girls began comparing Lisa's plans with her own celebration and criticizing what she thought was not up to par. The other people in the court started trickling away until no one came at all—except Elizabeth Martinez.

"I wondered why would they say yeah and then not show up," Lisa said. "Elizabeth was really into it. She was the only one who came to practice and paid for her dress. She was my best friend. The others, I thought they were going to be there for me, but they weren't. They let me down."

Lisa's mother, Graciela Alfaro, convinced her daughter that changing her plans and standing just with Elizabeth would be fine. And it was. Because not only was Lisa's quinceañera beautiful, but the experience, she said, made her stronger.

Chapter Seven &

A Bailar un Vals: *The Choreography*

> Then the girls and their escorts would perform a *quinceañera* waltz—a complicated dance to the "Blue Danube," which the kids had practiced once a week for the last three months. "The waltz is such a beautiful tradition," Mary Jo said. "It's what we have that makes the event really special. . . ."
>
> —*Susan Orlean*, Saturday Night

Laura Valenzuela had learned new dances thousands of times before. As a member of the Mexican Folkloric Dance Company of Chicago, her feet had tapped out the rhythms for presidents and the Pope. But never were the dances more important to her than the night of January 29, 1994. Never before did she so feel the music or her art celebrate life. Her life—her journey from a child to a young woman.

The specially crafted choreography that leads up to the quinceañera's waltz with her father can be a simple line dance or an elaborate ninety-minute dance-drama, complete with costumes, props, and sets. It all depends on the birthday girl and her family—what they want and what they can afford. And on her court—how much effort they put into rehearsals. For the kids in the court, the dance is the culmination of weeks of work and dedication. For the guests and family, it's the transforming moment, the moment that turns their little girl into la quinceañera.

FACING PAGE: *Karla Chavez leads her court in dance at her party in Houston, Texas.* —© 1996 F. Carter Smith

José Luis Ovalle, the dance company's artistic director, watched Valenzuela grow up from the age of five, when she followed her older sister into the company. The choreography for her debut was Ovalle's gift to Laura Valenzuela, a gift for which others pay at least $500.

In Miami, where quinces choreography is legendary, people look for someone who can put together a montage of dances. The guests are entertained by an opening number or two by the court of honor, and then by the entrance of the quinceañera herself. She dances one number with her father, then with her escort. And then she joins the court for several more numbers. Sometimes the choreography is an elaborate ballet created around a recent movie or a *telenovela* or the girl's life itself.

A Question of Style

The choreography—known in some areas as the *vals*—is your moment to shine. Every eye at every table in the room will be fixed on you. You'll want to give them something to look at. Something they will remember. Something that reflects you.

"Professional choreographers are hired to create themes," said Juan Muñoz of Miami. "In the Cuban and the Mexican traditions, they refer more to fantasy, like Cinderella or Sleeping Beauty. They may go to the extent of having a horse and chariot made. They turn out the lights, smoke clouds come out, there are lighting effects. It is a whole show. They would dance the waltz, the merengue, the salsa—it would last from twenty minutes to an hour, hour and a half, depending on how lavish the event was."

The more intricate you want the choreography to be, the more numbers you want to include, the more you'll need the services of a choreographer. As is the case with any professional, rates vary among choreographers. Their experience, the number of dances they are to create, and the number of rehearsals required all determine their price. A professional choreographer will charge anywhere from $300 for four numbers and a month's worth of rehearsals with the quinceañera and the court of honor to several thousand dollars to choreograph dances for a dozen songs and oversee four or five months of rehearsals.

If the services of a choreographer are too rich for your budget, a professional dancer with a folkloric company might be what you're looking for, someone who can teach the members of the court whatever dances you want. Their services may go for as little as $150. If the choreography is simple enough, the quinceañera herself may be able to work with a dance teacher or choreographer and then teach the court what she wants and run the rehearsals.

Benita Arevalo, who had a Tejano theme, knew that asking her court to perform a complicated *vals* might scare them off. "I wanted it simple, but I wanted it to look nice," she said. "I asked my court what they were willing to do. Some boys, if they think it's too complicated, they won't show."

For the first dance, Benita picked Garth Brooks's "Boot Scootin' Boogie," which by then had become so popular it had its own line dance. Bennie learned the dance from her gymnastics teacher at Barbara and Tammy's Dance Studio and then taught it to her court during five rehearsals.

Marisela Martinez also created her own simple choreography for her celebration, based on the advice of her sister and her experiences participating in other quinceañeras as a member of the court of honor. "We walked in and everyone got in a circle. We danced the entrance, and then my mom was dancing with my dad and me with my chambelán, and in the middle of the song, we switched partners, my mom danced with my chambelán and me with my dad," said Marisela. They danced to two more songs, finishing with Selena's "*Fotos y Recuerdos*," a cumbia she picked to get her guests in the mood to dance.

The Key Elements of Your Choreography

Whether it's simple or complex, every choreography has three parts.

THE ENTRANCE

Chivalry was alive and well when Nadia Ali's court entered the American Legion Hall in Bay Shore, New York, at her celebration. As the announcer introduced each couple, the

❦ ❦ La Marcha ❦ ❦

La marcha—the grand march—is a Mexican-American tradition in all the parts of the United States that once belonged to Mexico. Sometimes led by the court, sometimes led by the quinceañera and her parents, *la marcha* is a procession that includes the court, the immediate family, and the key, if not all of the, padrinos. They walk through the room, looping into circles and figure eights. It ends with everyone lined up for the choreography and presentation. "Every quinceañera celebration has the march, but they're all done differently," said Joe Duncan, the manager of El Tesoro Ballroom in San Antonio. "People come in and watch a quinceañera and see how others do it."

dama dropped a handkerchief. Her escort dropped to one knee, picked it up, and offered it to her. When she took it, he kissed her hand, arose, and led her to the front of the dance floor. When each couple took their place, they formed an arch, ready to greet Nadia, who walked in on the arms of her two brothers.

Lisa Alfaro's dama de honor, her padrinos, and her family walked in carrying lit candles, decorated with her colors, for their entrance. Fifteen people in all, they stood in a semicircle behind the chair where Lisa sat for her presentation.

A choreographer will sometimes have the court dance into the room. For Laura Valenzuela, Ovalle choreographed a dance that depicted the transition from a little girl to a teen. Teresa Perez's court danced into the room to a hip-hop number with heavy bass.

However you decide your court and family should come in, it's their moment in the spotlight. Their entrance anticipates your arrival and signals the guests that your big moment is almost at hand.

THE PRESENTATION

It is the magic moment, the defining moment, the moment everyone has waited for—la niña becomes una señorita. Her change in status is signaled in different ways for different heritages: her shoes may be changed from flats to heels; a crown of flowers or pearls may be changed to rhinestones; she will waltz with her father as her first dance of the evening. The quinceañera often does not appear at the reception until it is time for her presentation to her guests.

Presentations at Cuban quinceañeras are legendary. Some girls have made their debuts seated in a huge clamshell. Quinceañeras at Angelito's banquet hall in Hialeah, Florida, can arrive in an ornate pumpkin coach to rival that of any Cinderella.

Teresita Perez stood behind a carousel built on a revolving stage. When it came time for her debut, the stage rotated and there stood Teresita, who was greeted with the applause and cheers of her guests. Teresita's father led her down to the dance floor, where her court awaited her, each dama holding a red rose given to her by a flower girl. As Teresita passed each couple, the chambelán knelt and gave her the rose. As she reached the end of the dance floor, her bouquet of fifteen roses in hand, she curtsied to her guests. Teresita walked back to the stage and handed the roses to her mother, in anticipation of her dance with her father. She chose the song "My Havana" for her presentation, in homage to her Cuban heritage.

In some Latin cultures—Puerto Rican, Mexican, Salvadorean, Honduran, and Dominican among them—the quinceañera walks into the reception wearing flats. She walks to a chair in the middle of the dance floor, where her father or mother will change her shoes to heels, symbolizing her parents' recognition of her maturity. She literally changes from the shoes of a child to the shoes of a woman.

Celia Hernandez had worn a pearl headpiece throughout the day, but at her presentation, before her mother changed her shoes, Celia knelt on a pink satin pillow in the middle of the dance floor. The sponsors of the crown walked toward her, carrying their sparkling gift on a lacy, embroidered cushion. The madrina took the pearl headpiece off and replaced it with the rhinestone tiara.

THE WALTZ WITH PAPI

The presentation leads directly to the quinceañera's dance with her father—often, but not always, a waltz, but always a song that has great meaning for the quinceañera and her father. They dance together for at least part of the song. They are sometimes joined by her mother and the chambelán de honor, sometimes by the prince and princess; sometimes the court dances in a circle around them.

If the quinceañera's grandfather or even great-grandfather is alive, he dances with the quinceañera as well. Michele Nieto, who has nine uncles, also danced with each of them—now that she was a señorita.

The classic Mexican quinceañera choreography has four pieces of music and six parts. When the quinceañera appears at the reception, she first dances only with the damas in her court. In the second number, she dances with her father. The music stops while she sits in a chair. Her shoes are changed and the pearl or flower *tocado* (headpiece) is exchanged for the rhinestone crown. The music begins again and the chambelanes come in. The quinceañera dances with each one of them, and then finally with the chambelán de honor.

The waltz captures her social transition in dance, from a young girl frolicking with her contemporaries to a young woman who first dances with her father, then with boys her own age, and finally with her escort. As part of the transition, she is adorned with womanly shoes to take her first steps as a more mature person and crowned like a princess.

At some point in the presentation, the quinceañera curtsies to her guests. In San Antonio, Texas, Celia Hernandez waltzed first with her mother and then with her father. When the song ended, he led her to the six points of the dance floor, where Celia took a bit of her pink dress in each hand, raised the hooped skirt just the slightest bit, and curtsied to her guests at each point, after which her guests joined her on the dance floor and the ball began.

The Master of Ceremonies

The master of ceremonies, or announcer, weaves the musical numbers together into a spectacular entertainment for the guests, highlighting the guest of honor—la quinceañera. He or she is the glue that cements each part of the debut to the next. The announcer welcomes the guests to the reception and lets them know who the members of the court are and the "significance" of each element. It is often preferable to have a bilingual master of ceremonies to make sure everyone understands what is going on.

The party planner, choreographer, disc jockey, or lead singer of the band may all double as masters of ceremony, or they may bring a separate announcer with them. Either way, you have to provide the information so they can write a script tailored just for you. What do you want your guests to know about you? What are your favorite classes? Your hobbies? How do you like to spend your time? What is most important to you about this day?

If you prefer, you can write the script yourself and even ask someone in the family to be the announcer. Or ask someone in the family who knows you well to write the script and be the announcer as their gift to you.

Sometimes the announcer will tape-record best wishes from each of your parents, good friends, or family members who cannot attend to give them to you personally. Their comments can be played between the choreographed dances.

Talk with the master of ceremonies, asking to see scripts he or she has done in the past. Tell him or her what you do or do not want included. Make sure he or she has some information about each member of your court. As each person is announced, the guests will have a better idea of who they are

Music for the Waltz with Papi

Any Strauss waltz

"De Niña a Mujer" by Julio Iglesias

"Niña a Mujer" by Rod Nichols

"Mi Niña Bonita" by Tomás d'San Julian

"Niña" by Hugo Enrique

"Just Fifteen," title song, written and sung by David Hidalgo and Louis Perez

"Niña Mia"

"Daddy's Hands" by the Judds

"My Girl" by the Temptations

"Vals Fascinación" (Fascination)

"Theme from 'A Summer Place'"

"The Greatest Love of All" by Whitney Houston

"Alejandra"

"Rosalia"

"Dios Nunca Muere" (God Never Dies)

The Sleeping Beauty Waltz by Tchaikovsky

"Waltz of the Flowers" by Tchaikovsky

"Maria Elena"

The Princess Waltz

The Emperor Waltz

"Voices of Spring"

"Unforgettable" by Nat King Cole and his daughter, Natalie Cole

"Artist's Life"

"Daddy's Little Girl"

"Dulce Quinceañera"

Cumbia de Quinceañera

Vals de Mariposas

"Mi Ultima Muñeca"

§ § *Why the Waltz? The Mexican Version* § §

Even before the waltz came to Mexico at the end of the colonial period, girls were presented to society, according to José Luis Ovalle. Only the eldest daughter in families that did not have sons was presented, never the younger ones. "This caught on pretty fast, and the richest families in New Spain started doing this for each one of the daughters in the family, whether they had sons or not," Ovalle said. Once ballroom dancing crossed the ocean from Europe, it was incorporated into the presentation. "It became traditional to do choreography for a waltz where they would highlight the daughter," Ovalle said. "Then they did the *redova*, which is Polish in origin; the mazurka, and the polka, which is Czechoslovakian in origin; square dancing, which is English, and *chotis*, whose origin is Scottish.

"At the turn of the century, the waltzes were local competitions," Ovalle said. "That's why most of the waltzes created in Mexico have women's names—Julia, Alejandra, Maria Elena. They were created for the quinceañera."

beyond their name and why they are important to you. If you want music playing underneath what the announcer has to say, an instrumental works better than a song. It provides background music that enhances what the announcer is saying.

Hiring a Choreographer

Rosendo Ramon is a well-known choreographer in the Miami area. "Every quinces is a little bit different, because I think that every quinceañera is a little bit different," said Ramon. "So I try to build their taste—what they like, what they don't like—into the choreography."

Ramon sits down with the girl and her mother early on, and the three just talk about what they want. What kind of songs? How many will there be? How large is the court? Do they have experience dancing to the kind of music the quinceañera wants? Who are

*M*ireya Cantu, of Salt Lake City, Utah, is forever captured as a fairy princess in her formal quinceañera portrait.
—Don Polo Video and Photo

*P*atricia Correa puts the finishing touches on her makeup the morning of her quinceañera. —Pilsen Photo Studio

*K*arla Chavez beams with delight as Josy, her mother (right), and a friend arrange each curl just so. —©1996 F. Carter Smith

*W*hile her mother helps fasten her dress, Karla Chavez looks behind her for reassurance as the moment of her celebration nears. —©1996 F. Carter Smith

The Reverend David Zapalac congratulates Karla at her quinceañera mass, held at St. Ann's Roman Catholic Church in Houston, Texas. —©1996 F. Carter Smith

A solemn moment during Karla's quinceañera mass, during which she renews her baptismal vows. —© 1996 F. Carter Smith

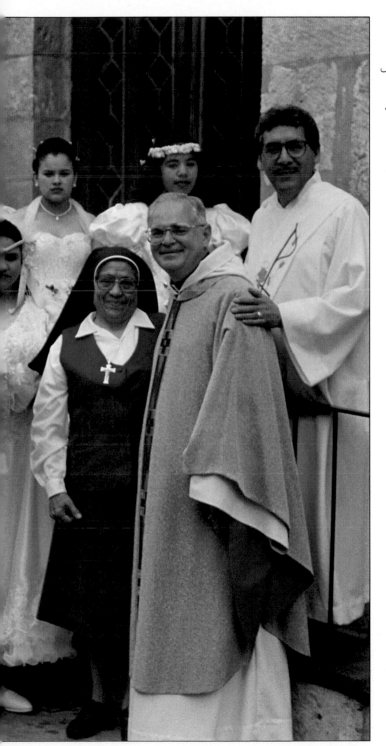

Millions of viewers throughout the world saw these quinceañeras honored during the annual group mass held at San Fernando Cathedral in San Antonio. The celebration, held each May, occurred during the Spanish Mass transmitted by satellite all over the globe. ——Courtesy of San Fernando Cathedral

ABOVE: *Courts of escorts are becoming more popular among Mexican Americans, just as they have been in Mexico for a number of years. Sandra Delgado Martínez stands with her court, which she recruited from a local military academy in Mexico City.*

LEFT: *Fourteen girls, one for each year of life, form a traditional court of honor and stand beside la quiceañera for their formal portrait in a bucolic setting. Their dresses are a variation of the quinceañera's dress, which has an overskirt that can be removed for the dance later in the evening.*

Lori Hernandez is greeted by her mother, Sylvia, and the cousins and friends who stood in her court of honor after the mass at Our Lady of Guadalupe Catholic Church in Lubbock, Texas. Her bouquet of silk flowers symbolizes her new commitment and responsibility to the community and to God. She wears a crown in triumph over sin through leading a Christian life. Her grandmother stitched and beaded her dress. —Sharon M. Steinman

*I*ncluding as many young children as possible in a court of honor brings the extended family together. Here the young cousins of the Pérez González family pose in a corner of a Mexico City garden during a reception.

La niña traditionally transforms into una señorita as she waltzes with her father. Jesus Romero of Freeport, New York, did the honor twice at the celebration for his twin daughters, Jessica and Jarlyn. —©1995 Newsday

After dancing with their father, the twins are free to dance with anyone at the party. Here one twin dances with a member of their court, while a guest enjoys the company of the other. —©1995 *Newsday*

*T*he carousel delighted Teresita Perez's guests at her quinces celebration in Hialeah, Florida. When the carousel rotated, Teresita, who was standing behind it, came into view, to cheers and applause of her guests. Her father, Oscar, led her off the stage and to the center of the dance floor for the waltz. ——Panorama Photo Studio and Video Productions

*C*andlelight ceremonies are traditionally part of many quinceañera celebrations. Each girl in Teresita Perez's court holds a decorated candle for her to blow out, giving her a chance to make fifteen wishes. ——Panorama Photo Studio and Video Productions

*L*ynette Bedoya beams as the center of attention, while her parents, Raul and Edith, and her entire court lead a toast with the glasses especially decorated for the occasion. Behind them is a silver curtained stage and the shimmering shell from which Lynette appeared for her presentation in Miami. ——Enrique Muñoz Studio

the men in the family she wants to dance with—just her father? Or her grandfather, godfather, and uncles as well? Are there other special family touches the quinceañera and her mother want included? Is there a theme? What style dress does the quinceañera plan to have? Has she already bought it? Where will the party be? Are there balconies to enter and exit from? How large is the dance floor? Will sets be needed? All those factors and more affect how the choreographer creates the steps for the dances and how the dance and presentation will ultimately look.

When looking for a choreographer, talk with as many candidates as you can. Among the questions you should ask are: Will he or she have the music recorded, so it plays through from beginning to end? Or will the disc jockey have to mix each number into the next? Who picks the music? How does he or she choreograph the music? How many rehearsals do you require? If you did not find the choreographer through a recommendation, ask for references.

Talking to them, you'll learn what they can offer you and in the process refine your ideas of what you want. See how they respond to your ideas. If they don't like the music you've chosen or if they insist on their own music or their own themes, keep looking for someone who is more willing to work with you, to craft the celebration you want, not the celebration they've done hundreds of times before.

What the quinceañera picks for her music often depends on her cultural background. Some girls simply want a traditional waltz. If they're Puerto Rican, they may want a waltz, some salsa, and a traditional ballad to dance with her father. If she's Dominican, she may select a merengue, a waltz, and the dance with her father.

Just as today's quinceañera lives in different times from her mother and grandmother, so the music she dances to at her debut is different. "Quinceañeras want something modern," said Rosendo Ramon. "There are a lot of choreographers out there who have been doing this for twenty, thirty years. They don't go to clubs, they don't see what's happening. They stick with what they know and what they've taught for twenty years. A lot of quinceañeras now want modern steps, modern music."

Choreographers charge by the number of dances they have to craft and how complicated those dances are. Whenever you rehearse, the choreographer will be there to help the court through the steps, to make sure your presentation looks just the way you want it.

The Importance of Rehearsals

Where to Find a Choreographer

In local Latino newspapers
and magazines

Banquet hall managers

Record stores

Bridal shop managers and owners

Disc jockeys

Party planners and coordinators

Families who have thrown quince años
celebrations

Local cultural societies

Local folkloric dance companies

Quinceañera cake bakers

The choreographer will devise a rehearsal schedule, depending on how many numbers you want to perform with your court. The more dedicated the group is to learning the dances, the more confidence they'll have at the party and the better the dances will be.

The general rule of thumb is one week of rehearsal for each musical number to be danced. If you have eight dances to learn, the choreographer will probably schedule eight weeks of rehearsal. "If the kids know how to dance, things move a little faster because I have less teaching to do," said Rosendo Ramon. "But if I see in the first practices that they need more help, I'll schedule more practices here and there."

Having the choreographer dance in the court or having the oldest couple act as leaders often helps the younger, less confident members of the court learn the dances. When one of the chambelanes dropped out of Teresita Perez's court at the last minute, her mother replaced him with Rosendo Ramon, the choreographer!

Relying on the older members of the court to set the example for the younger members can make the rehearsals go more smoothly. And the parents themselves can lend a hand, helping to teach the dance steps and turning the rehearsals themselves into parties, once the work is done.

Esthersita Penton Nodarse, who has twenty years of experience planning quinceañeras among Miami's Cuban community, advises parents to carefully plan the rehearsals right down to the transportation. In Miami, the family hosts a rehearsal dinner, and for each night of practice, snacks are served for the court and whoever else comes as well. Making the rehearsals fun will help you meet the challenge of getting the members of the court to the practices. People will inevitably skip some rehearsals, and sometimes, especially if the quinceañera herself is teaching the choreography and running the rehearsals, no one may show up. "It worried me," said Fanny Padilla, who choreographed her own quinceañera in Chicago, "when people skipped the rehearsals. But everything came out all right in the end."

Marisela Martinez said she had to keep reminding herself to be patient with her court. "I know that no one's perfect and everyone's not going to go to practice every day. You have to be prepared. Very prepared."

Marisela, Fanny, and Benita Arevalo all grew from choreographing their own *valses.* They learned to organize the rehearsals so the court had enough time to learn the dances. And they learned management skills, to get people to cooperate and work together toward a common goal, making each other—and especially the quinceañera— look good on her special night.

Finally, after weeks of work, it's time for the dress rehearsal at the reception site. The dress rehearsal will give you a chance to see how the choreography will look on the dance floor itself and to make any last-minute adjustments. If you've been practicing in your living room, for example, and the dance floor is larger, the dress rehearsal will give you and the court a chance to get used to the additional room.

You'll find out what the rehearsal policy is when you contract for the reception site. Some places will let you rehearse all you want, as long as you call the manager in advance. Other places only include one rehearsal in the rental price. Make sure to ask when you negotiate the contract for the reception site. If one rehearsal is not enough on the stage or dance floor where the choreography will ultimately be performed, ask the site manager if you can have access on more than one night. If you are working with a choreographer, be clear during your first interviews how much access to the reception site you'll have before the party.

Choreography Ideas

There are as many themes as there are quinceañeras. Think of what your fantasy is and find a choreographer who can make it come true. Your court is there to help you, to be the characters with whom you want to surround yourself. They are there to help you tell your story through dance.

◆ A large box is onstage or brought to the middle of the floor where the court is dancing. When it opens, out fly balloons, and then the quinceañera herself comes out.

◆ For a court of all chambelanes, a card table is brought onto the stage or dance floor, and the chambelanes are playing cards. The quinceañera appears and dances the tango with each one. They start fighting over her, but in the end, she vanquishes them all.

◆ If the quinceañera wants to be a model, she may make her presentation seated in a large picture frame and then walk through to her audience.

◆ Several choreographers have included the presentation of flowers to the quinceañera during the waltz. Sometimes the flower girl enters with a basket of long-stemmed roses and presents each one to the damas. During the choreography, they give the rose to the quinceañera, who enters with one herself, so that she has a bouquet of fifteen.

◆ If Cinderella is the theme, the court dances as though they are at a ball. The quinceañera wanders in dressed in rags, stunned. She walks behind a booth, where dressers are on hand to help her change from rags into her beautiful quinceañera dress and crown—to become the princess at the ball. Her escort, of course, is the prince.

◆ The Little Mermaid inspires a nautical theme for the decorations, favors, and invitations. The quinceañera wears a fishtail-hem dress and appears on a clamshell.

◆ In Phoenix, a ninety-minute choreography depicted a girl's life from childhood to her quinceañera. Not only did the court participate, but so did her parents. Costume changes depicted the various stages of her life.

❦ ❦ *A Dominican Tradition* ❦ ❦

For an old Santo Domingo theme, the dance floor was transformed into the plaza. The damas wore wide-brimmed hats and carried fans and parasols. In the center of the floor stood a maypole bedecked with ribbons that matched the colors of their dresses. Each color symbolized a wish for the quinceañera—peace, faith, love, joy, and hope, for example. As each person grabbed a ribbon, she or he made their wish—the girls saying theirs in Spanish and the boys in English. During the dance, they wove in and out, and wove the ribbons around the pole.

Chapter Eight ❦
Music

> While the music played, no one stopped dancing. That's why people didn't
> want to leave, because of the music.
>
> —*Fanny Padilla, speaking of her quinceañera*

F elicia Aguirre and her mother listened to bands at weddings. They listened to
bands at quinceañeras. For five months, they listened to bands whenever and wherever they could. Still Felicia could not find a band she liked.

" 'No, I don't like this. No, I don't like this.' I said you need to make up your mind
because we can't just get a band in one day," said her mother, Rita.

You may have all the songs picked for the choreography, but you have only begun the
search for one of the most important elements of your celebration—the music.

"Music is only one ingredient in a successful party, but like the other ingredients, it
has its value, its point, its moment," said Andres Trujillo, who plays violin and piano
duets with his wife, Darlene, and is also part of an orchestra called Almendra in the
Miami area. "Each party, each hour needs some planning, some time."

FACING PAGE: *Mariachis serenade Karla Chavez at her quinceañera party in Houston.*—© 1996 F. Carter
Smith

Something for Everyone

Strains of music woven throughout the day can set the mood and serve as a transition from one element to the next. An organist or guitarist playing as the guests arrive for a church service can set a reverent tone, while a pianist and violinist playing while people arrive at the reception can invite the guests into a room with a romantic bolero. A lively merengue or mambo will get people on the dance floor and will not let them sit down until a slow dance is played so the guests can catch their breath.

Begin by breaking down the day into segments, from the various parts of the church service to the different elements of the reception. Which parts would you like music played for? What kind of music would you like? Even if a full choir and a chamber orchestra are too rich for your budget, you can have the music you want played by a disc jockey.

Meet with the musicians or disc jockeys you are interviewing for your celebration and be frank with them about what you would like to hear, what songs have special meaning for your family. Disc jockeys often invite potential clients to see them at work at a quinceañera, and live musicians will play for people who may hire them so their potential customers can hear part of their repertoire and their sound. If there is a song that was special to the quinceañera as a young child or a member of the family has composed a piece and you want it played, ask the musicians whether they can learn it. But do not feel that you need to come to a meeting with the musicians or disc jockey with a full playlist of songs that will fill the entire night. The musicians are there to create a mood and keep the party moving. They will be ready to offer suggestions.

Our cultures have identifiable music styles and forms that appeal to our emotions. Ideally, the music should appeal to as broad a range of people as we invite: something our grandparents can relate to, something our children can relate to, something our brother-in-law from Argentina is familiar with, something our *bistío* Carlos remembers from his youth in Havana. The smart musician or disc jockey in larger metropolitan areas, such as New York, Miami, or Los Angeles, will ask about the cultural backgrounds of the guests. "We'll ask if everyone's Cuban or if they're going to invite many Anglos, or if there are guests who are Peruvian, Venezuelan, Mexican, or Colombian," said Andres. "We try to play music for everyone who comes. If we're hired by an Ecuadoran, they'll invite Ecuadorans and so we have to know something that's Ecuadoran; if they invite Venezuelans, we have to know something Venezuelan; if they invite Brazilians, we have to know something Brazilian. Generally, that's all part of our repertory, music from all countries. And not just music you've heard, but something that's folkloric, that people identify with their home country. The idea isn't only to perform well, but so the people themselves will say to other people, 'The music was fabulous.' "

Finding the band or disc jockey that has the breadth to entertain everyone, no matter what their age or background, is no small task. Selecting who will play for the dance can be nerve-racking. You have to go out and listen to bands and disc jockeys at work to find one that's within your budget and that has a repertory that everyone can relate to. If you hire a band that only plays what the quinceañera and her friends want, the adults will not have a very good time, because they cannot relate to the music. If you hire someone who only plays tangos and boleros, the kids will be bored out of their minds. The key is to find someone that has a broad enough repertoire or library to appeal to everyone.

Some Miami families get around the generation gap by hiring a disc jockey for the kids and a band for the adults, so the music never stops, said Juan Muñoz. "The bands usually are for the hot salsa and the top forty merengue, and the DJ is for the top forty, the things you play on the radio and whatever is current," said Muñoz. "It's a lot more fun for the grown-ups and for the kids."

No matter what section of the celebration you hire a musician for, the average price for their services is $100 per hour per musician, whether it's a string quartet, an organist, or a marimba band. You can expect to pay between $500 and $2,000. Disc jockeys command a wider range, anywhere between $150 and $1,500, depending on the number of hours, the lighting set-up, and any special effects you want, such as smoke or bubble machines. Musicians are in high demand during the holiday season, from November 1 to January 12. Their prices rise as much as 50 to 100 percent during that time of year.

As in the case of the other professionals, the sooner you decide whom you want to hire and put down a deposit, the better your chances are of getting the music you want on your special day. Generally, six months before the celebration is more than adequate. Most musicians will book at the last minute if they have the date open. But why take the chance?

There are three areas of the celebration that traditionally call for music, for which you may want to hire musicians or a disc jockey.

The Church

If you are having a religious service, talk with the priest or minister about the music you want played during the ceremony. He or she not only will tell you what is appropriate, but also will put you in touch with the music director. Sometimes the church fee covers an organist or pianist, but not always. You may have to pay extra, usually between $100 and $200.

A month or two after you book the church, the music director can help you select the music for your service and advise you of any liturgical restrictions. If you want something other than what the church usually offers—a choir, a violin, mariachis, a harp or piano in addition to the organ—the music director can help you make the arrangements and may recommend musicians if you need them.

In churches that offer only group quinceañera services, you may want to pool your resources with the parents of the other girls to pay for mariachis, a choir, or any musicians beyond what the church usually offers.

The Reception: Cocktails and Dinner

As your guests arrive at the party, you may want to welcome them with the strains of strings. "If you're going to chat with someone, you don't want to hear boom, boom, boom in the back," said Darlene Trujillo. "You want music that's pretty, agreeable, that's not really loud, and that everyone likes."

The music that greets the guests when they arrive should entice them, invite them into the room. A soft, classical piece, like a Bach chorale, will draw people into the room, because the music is so sweet and soothing. By varying the tempo and mood of the music, the musicians will entertain your guests. If you hire string musicians to play during the cocktail hour, do not expect them to be able to play for the dance. They do not have a big enough sound.

The Dance

Hiring the music for the dance can be one of the biggest areas of contention between the quinceañera and her parents. She and her friends want the music they listen and dance to, but the parents and older relatives want their kind of dance music, with lyrics that are familiar or that they can at least understand. You have to find someone who can do it all so that everyone has a good time.

Just as you want a softer sound during the reception, so people can chat without straining, you want a bigger sound for the dance, a sound that fills the room, a sound that a DJ with professional equipment or a full band or orchestra can provide. And most of the music played should be familiar to the guests, not what the disc jockey is into or original songs the band wants to showcase.

You may want the band or DJ to play the songs for your *vals* and presentation. If you are doing your own choreography and have particular songs in mind, talk with the band or DJ to make sure they have the music you want. Make sure they will rehearse with you a few days before your party. Ask if this is included in their fee or whether you have to pay extra.

Often the decision to hire a DJ or a band comes down to two things: personal preference and price.

Going Live: Hiring a Band

There is nothing quite like the excitement and festive feeling a live band generates. They not only get people out on the dance floor and moving, but also give the guests a chance to hear interpretations of popular songs with the creativity and musicianship only a live performance brings.

A band's best advertising is often word of mouth. Keep your ears open at weddings and other quinceañera celebrations you may attend and ask for a business card from the band leader before you leave. Band members themselves are very conscious of the fact that they are not only playing a party but are also showcasing their talents for guests who may be planning a party of their own.

Catering hall managers, dressmakers, party coordinators, photographers, and videographers—any of the party professionals you are working with may have bands they can recommend. Local shopping publications, churches, and community bulletin boards may be good sources as well. Bands often showcase at bridal shows and expos as well as in bridal advertising supplements inserted in newspapers and distributed through retailers in the wedding and party industry. Bands can be found in the yellow pages of large metropolitan areas and through booking agents. Because of the special elements of a quinceañera— with the presentation, the waltz, the choreography, for example—it's a good idea to hold out for a band who has played at quinceañeras before, or you'll find yourself having to explain the format, the traditions, and what is appropriate and what is not.

Working with a booking agent is often the most efficient way of finding a band, but you will pay a 20 percent premium for the service. An agent can save you a lot of legwork because he or she has a number of bands they can offer you. Because the agent has a reputation to maintain, he or she will ensure the band shows up. "We save them money, because a lot of times the band leader will say, 'how much do you want to pay.' Whatever figure the person says is what the band charges, whether they're worth that amount or not," said Albert Esquival, a booking agent in San Antonio.

The agent's commission works like this: If a band's fee is $1,000, you pay the $200 commission up front, when you sign the contract with the booking agent. That money also serves as a deposit, to lock in the date you want the band to play. The agent keeps half the deposit and gives half to the band. The balance is due in cash or a cashier's check at the party.

Family and friends can be excellent sources for recommendations for bands. People you know have already heard and liked whatever group they are recommending enough to tell you about them. But be sure to talk with the person who hired the group as well as the one who organized the celebration, just to make sure things ran smoothly. Marisela Martinez found the band that played at her party through her boyfriend. And she got a bonus: they brought another band with them, one that was just starting out, to play when the first band went on a break. Because they booked through Marisela's boyfriend, the band gave them a discount on their fee. Essentially, the Martinezes were able to hire two bands for $800, Marisela said. And they also had a DJ to fill in when both bands were on break.

When the Padillas started looking around for a band for their daughter Fanny's party in Chicago, they contacted someone at the church, who knew of a group for $1,300. That was more than they wanted to spend, so they found another band at a wedding they went to, one that also brought a backup band to play during the breaks, for $750.

"They were the only ones that did that," said Concepcion Padilla, Fanny's father. "Most of the bands would put on a cassette when they took a break, but this group brought along another band, to give them some exposure and to keep the party moving."

And move it did. At the end of the night, no one wanted to leave. "While the music played, no one stopped dancing," said Fanny. The name of the band was Ingratitud, said Concepcion Padilla. "But we were in gratitude to them because they were terrific and didn't cost much."

For Flexibility and Economy: Choose a Disc Jockey

The disc jockey has one job all night—to keep the dance floor packed. If he is playing one song after another and no

Tips for Hiring a Band

♦ See the band play at a quinceañera before you hire them: Were they entertaining? Were they on time? Did they look clean and sharp? Were they responsive to the crowd? Was the lead singer a good MC? Did they know the elements of the quinces?

♦ Make sure they are interested in giving you what you want, not merely showcasing their original stuff.

♦ Avoid a band whose members are too young or who do not have much experience by asking for and checking their references.

♦ Use any connections you have—in-laws, coworkers, neighbors, church groups—to find a band.

♦ Be honest about your price range. If you are dealing directly with a band that is more expensive than you can afford, sometimes they will negotiate. If you are dealing with a booking agent, they will get you the most value for your money.

♦ Make sure that even if the band takes a break, they have cassette music, or even a backup band to keep the music going and the dance floor filled.

♦ Ask to see their song list. Don't be afraid to suggest songs you want them to play so you and your guests have a good time.

♦ If a member of your family likes to get up and sing—your grandfather or a three-year-old sister who thinks she is Selena—ask the band when you first talk with them if they will back them up on a particular song. If they say no, look for a new band. "It's more fun for the whole family," said Ramiro Burr. "Even if they can't sing, it doesn't matter. The point is, it's a family event."

one is dancing, he is not doing his job. Disc jockeys can play music for all tastes and all generations. Even though hiring Gloria Estefan, Wili Chilín, or La India to perform at a quinceañera would be unthinkably expensive, all of them could sing at your celebration—through the skilled sound mixing of a disc jockey. And most of them come with lights, smoke, even bubbles—the tools to turn a dance floor into a disco. Just as the lead singer in a band doubles as the master of ceremonies, the disc jockey keeps the party going not only through the music he plays but also through the skills he brings as an announcer.

And it's important to see a disc jockey in action at a quince años celebration before you hire him. Joe "Pepe" Sanchez is a disc jockey and professional radio announcer with twenty years' experience—and bookings three years in advance. His philosophy is simple: "We're there for the people," said Sanchez. "We make them feel good. We make them dance. We'll say, 'If there's something you want, let us know.' "

Sanchez warns people to beware of disc jockeys who charge high prices and give little service. "Then there are the guys who want to play what they have and not what people want. I cater to people, whatever they want. It's their night. They're paying for it."

The Romantic Effect: Mariachis

The mariachis were made for serenading señoritas and who better to serenade with "Las Mañanitas," the traditional birthday song, than la quinceañera? Most often the mariachis—the Mexican string and trumpet musicians who sport broad-brimmed hats and charro costumes bedecked with gleaming silver—play during the two-hour reception, the cocktail hour, and the dinner.

The roots of the mariachis go back more than four hundred years, but it is only since the mid-1990s that those origins were definitively traced to Cocula, Jalisco, a village located about twenty miles west of Guadalajara and Lake Chapala, by Efraín de la Cruz, a journalist for the Guadalajara daily *El Informador*, in his book *El Origen del Mariachi Coculense.* The indigenous Coca tribe had a rich musical culture when the Franciscan missionaries arrived in the area around 1530. The missionaries saw the musical background as a means to convert the Cocas to Christianity and asked the viceroy to send indigenous musicians from the Colegio de Tlatelolco, where they had learned Spanish music. They did, and the *mestizaje*—the mix of the two cultures—produced musicians who played guitars, pipes, and a box drum in honor of the area's patron saints, Saint Michael and the Virgin Mary, in a festival held on September 29. That festival is held to this day.

Through the intervening centuries, the mariachi roamed the hills of Jalisco looking for food and work. De la Cruz, who has studied the mariachis for more than thirty-five years, traces the word to the Coca language, which comes from Nahuatl, and means song and joy. The word *mariachi*, de la Cruz writes, is believed to have derived from the lines of "Maria Ce Son," a song praising the Virgin Mary, which is today known as "María del Río." The traditional mariachi is a string ensemble of two violins, a guitar, a guitarrón, and a vihuela. It was embraced by politicians and revolutionaries alike around the turn of the century. In 1940, the mariachi added trumpets. It became even more popular through the films of Jorge Negrete, Pedro Infante, and Vicente Fernández, eventually becoming synonymous with Mexico.

Tips for Hiring a DJ

• Ask to see the DJ in action before the debut, so you can see the equipment, how he works in a similar setting to the one you have planned, and how the crowd responds to him.

• What kind of sound equipment does he or she use? Stay away from DJs who use home stereo equipment. Home equipment may be fine for your backyard barbecue, but you need power only professional equipment can provide to fill a large room and a dance floor packed with people.

• Ask where he or she has used the equipment on a job. How many people did the place hold?

• What kind of lights and special effects does he or she have? Are they extra or included in the cost?

• Is the DJ's library big enough and varied enough to suit everyone? What type of music does he or she provide? Does the DJ play vinyl, tape, or CD?

• What is the fee? How many hours does this cover? What is the overtime charge?

• How long does it take to set up? How much space and what kind of power source does he or she need? What kind of plugs? Does the DJ provide adapters?

• If you want a special song played—especially if you have something particular in mind for the choreography—does the DJ have it? Can he or she get it? It should be part of the DJ's business to provide that music.

• Has the DJ played a quinceañera before? Can he or she provide references?

In Miami, the mariachis have a seller's market. While the mariachis in Chicago, which has a large Mexican population, get between $400 and $600 an hour, Miami's mariachis charge $500 *per song*. The demand for mariachis is so great that non-Mexicans don the distinctive charro costumes, take up the traditional instruments, and play, prompting some groups to advertise as *legítimo Mexicano*—true Mexicans. Because they are so expensive in Miami, most people hire the mariachis to serenade la quinceañera with two or three songs, one of which is always "Las Mañanitas."

If the mariachis are hired to stay through the reception, they will serenade la quinceañera first and then stroll from table to table, taking requests, then serenade la quinceañera one last time before leaving.

Families that have a church service for their daughters sometimes hire mariachis to serenade la quinceañera when she arrives at the church. Others have mariachis play during the service, and "Las Mañanitas" is sung at the end by everyone, just before they leave the church.

Because mariachis are in such demand, they may play several parties in one night. Be very sure about when you want them to come and how long you want them to play. Their schedules often do not allow for much adjustment.

You can find mariachis through the local paper, through bridal consultants, booking agents, and by word of mouth. Make sure to get references and to check them. They usually require half their payment the day they commit to play at your party, and the remainder in cash the night of the celebration.

Contracts

Whether you hire strolling musicians, a band, or a DJ, having a contract is as much in your best interest as theirs. The contract, which is signed when the deposit is paid, guarantees that the band is booked to show up on the date, at the time and place that you want.

The deposits run anywhere from 20 to 50 percent of the musicians' fee. The remainder is due at the party, most often in cash. The contract will specify when the balance is due and how, whether in cash or certified check.

Las Mañanitas

Estas son las mañanitas,
De que cantaba el rey David.
Hoy por ser tu quince años
Te las cantamos así.

These are the morning songs
That King David used to sing.
Since today's your fifteenth birthday
We serenade you this way.

Despierta, mi bien, despierta
Mira, que ya amaneció,
Ya los pajaritos cantan,
La luna ya se metió.

Awaken, my love, awaken
Look, the dawn is already here,
The birds are already singing,
And the moon has just set.

Que linda esta la mañana
En que vengo a saludarte.
Venimos todos con gusto
Y placer a felicitarte.

How beautiful is this morning
On which I've come to greet you.
We all come with pleasure
and more pleasure to congratulate you.

El día en que tu naciste
Nacieron todas las flores.
En la pilar del bautismo
Cantaron los ruiseñores.

The day that you were born,
All the flowers were created.
On the baptismal fount
The nightingales sang.

Ya viene amaneciendo
Ya la luz del día nos vió.
Levantarte de mañana
Mira, que ya amaneció.

The dawn is already coming,
And day's light has already seen us.
Arise this morning
Look, the dawn has already broken.

Si yo pudiera bajarte
Las estrellas y un lucero
Para poder demostrarte
Lo mucho que yo te quiero.

If I could I would bring down
The stars, including a bright one,
So I could show you
How much it is I love you.

Quisiera ser un San Juan,
Quisiera ser un San Pedro
Para venirte a cantar
Con la música del cielo.

I would like to be Saint John,
I would like to be Saint Peter
To come with heavenly music
To sing to you.

Con jasmines y flores
Este día quiero adornar,
Hoy por ser tus quince años
Que venimos a cantar.

With jasmine and with flowers
I want to adorn this day,
Today, being your fifteenth birthday,
Which is why we've come to sing.

WHAT TO INCLUDE IN THE CONTRACT

- The date, time, and place of the party.
- How long the DJ or musicians are to play, the start time, and the end time.
- How many breaks the DJ or musicians will get. Will they get a fifteen-minute break for every forty-five minutes they play? Will they play two hours and then get a thirty-minute break and play another two hours?
- The total sum of money due, how much is paid on deposit.
- When the balance is due and in what form—cash, cashier's check, credit card.
- The amount they charge per hour if the dance goes beyond what you have contracted.
- Your name, address and telephone number.
- The name, address, and telephone number of the musicians or DJ, including a number where they can be reached the day of the party.
- The name, address, and telephone number of the booking agent or party planner or whoever booked the band or DJ.
- Is there an extra charge if they have to haul the equipment up stairs or if the parking is farther away than they thought?
- Does the DJ or someone in the band act as the master of ceremonies during the reception?
- If you are concerned about the DJ or band bringing a big entourage, ask whom they will bring besides themselves. If you are concerned about the number in their crew, specify who they can bring in the contract.
- Be up-front with the DJ or band about where you want them to play. They will bring the equipment they need to give you the best sound and you will have a better party.

CANCELING THE CONTRACT

It is very important to specifically include in the contract the acceptable reasons for canceling the party and your obligation to the musicians or disc jockey. Unless the contract specifies when you get the deposit back, you will see your money again for few reasons short of a death in the immediate family.

Among the areas that should be covered in the contract are what happens if the band breaks up before the date they are to play for you. If you have dealt directly with them, you should get your money back. But if you have hired them through a booking agent or a party planner, give them a chance to find a replacement that satisfies you. If they cannot, they should refund your money and cancel the contract.

The grace period you have to cancel the contract should be specified in the written agreement, as should the acceptable reasons for canceling. Otherwise, you may leave yourself open for the musicians or booking agent to sue you for breach of contract.

❧ ❧ *Where to Find Musicians* ❧ ❧

Booking agents

Local orchestra members

Churches

The yellow pages

Party planners and consultants

Catering halls

Local newspapers and magazines

Bridal shops

Record stores

Radio stations

Friends and relatives

How to Know If a Booking Agent Is Legit

- How long has he been in business? Does he or she have a permanent office? Beware of agents who work out of their apartments.
- Can he or she give you recommendations from recent quinceañeras where his bands have played?
- What bands has he booked for the weekend? Can you see them play?
- Avoid people who moonlight as agents. Their *day* job should be booking bands, not their sideline.
- Call a local radio station to see if they have heard of the agent.
- Call the local Better Business Bureau to see if they have any complaints against the agent on file.
- If you are from out of town, talk to someone where the agent is to see what kind of reputation they have.

Before you sign, find out what happens to your deposit if one of the band members gets sick, or they have a flat and come later than you wanted them, or if they get into an accident and cannot come at all. Do you get all your deposit back? Some of it? Will they find a replacement band or disc jockey at no charge to you? Make sure their answers to these questions are incorporated into the contract.

Some Ideas for Quinceañera Recordings

RECORDS

"Quinceañera," on *De Pachanga con los Dinners,* recorded by Los Dinners. Harmony, 1977

"La Quinceañera," on *Epoca de Oro de los Graduados* by Los Graduados. Opa Locka, Florida: Sonotone Music Corporation, 1987.

"Quinceañera," on *Contestación a la Banda del Carro Rojo* by Los Terribles. Carino Records, 1976.

"Quinceañera" by Barros on *The Wonderful Latin-American Sound of Colombia.* RCA International, 1968.

"La Quinceañera" by Tito Puente on *Poli Chavez y Sus Coronados en San Diego.* San Diego, California: Pocha Records, 1979.

"Linda Quinceañera," on *Conjunto Acapulco Tropical,* recorded by Conjunto Acapulco Tropical. RCA/Ariola, 1985.

CASSETTE

"Quinceañera" on *En Su Mayor Momento,* recorded by Caña Brava. New York: Platano Records, distributed by Antilla Records, 1995.

"Quinceañera" by Alvaro Davila and Memo Mendez on *Grandes Exitos de Telenovela.* Fonovisa, 1994 (also available on CD).

"Quinceañera," on *Salsa y Merengue—¡Que Rico!* recorded by Ocho de Colombia. Miami, Florida: Sonotone Music Corporation, 1990.

"La Quinceañera," on *Quince Exitos de Los Tam y Tex,* recorded by Tam y Tex. Houston, Texas: distributed by Ramex Records, 1987.

"Quinceañera," on *Quince Exitos con Los Dandys,* recorded by Los Dandys. RCA, 1983.

Solo para Quinceañeras: 20 Exitos (20 hits). Includes "Baila Quinceañera," "Quinceañera," "Felicidad," "Niña de Quince Años," and more. Miami, Florida: TH-MEX, distributed by TH-Rodven, 1989.

"Quinceañera," on *El Baile,* recorded by Wilfrido Vargas. Opa Locka, Florida: Sonotone, 1987.

"Quinceañera," on *Los Grandes Exitos de los Dandys.* RCA International, 1988.

COMPACT DISC

"Quinceañera" by Vidal-Mendoza on *Música Tropical de Colombia.* Medellín, Colombia: Discos Fuentes, 1992.

"Quinceañera," on *Banda America,* recorded by Banda America. Miami, Florida: Sony Discos. 1994.

Quinceañera. Includes "The Blue Danube," "Tales from the Vienna Woods," "Voices of Spring," and four others, recorded by the National Philharmonic Orchestra. Orfeon, 1989.

"Quinceañera," on *Pétalos y Espinas,* recorded by Yonics. Mexico: Fono Visa-Melody, 1987 (also available on cassette).

SHEET MUSIC

Album de Valses Venezolanos by José María Tortolero. Madrid: Afrodisio Aguado, 1989.

Danzas para Piano by José Liciano Quiñones. Puerto Rico: Instituto de Cultura Puertorriqueña, División de Música, 1987.

Chapter Nine

Fashion Confection: The Dresses and Other Attire

The girls, some of them want a sexy dress, but they know that their parents or their godparents want them to have a more traditional style. When they try on the more traditional dress, they see they look like Cinderella.

—*Paulette Peace, owner, Elegant Touch Bridals, Brentwood, New York*

While the quinceañera's mother is trying to find the best deal on the hall, meet whatever requirements the church may have, and keep a million details under control, one and only one subject captures the quinceañera: the dress. Long and full, glittering with pearls, and dusted with sequins, the dress transforms la niña beyond a señorita and into a real-life fairy princess. While the entire celebration is a collaboration between mother and daughter, this is especially true of the dress.

Most of the girls start their search for their dream dress by scouring the bridal magazines for ideas. But a quinceañera dress is not a wedding dress, although it is often white and lacy. Traditionally a quinceañera wears a floor-length ball gown, full in the skirt and fitted in the bodice. It may be pink or another pastel, plain white, or white trimmed with the colors worn by the court of honor.

When you shop for a dress, be sure to try on all the trappings that go with it—the

FACING PAGE: *Yolanda Aceves of Salt Lake City, Utah, chose to wear white for her celebration, trimmed with the color worn by her court.* —Don Polo Video and Photo

crown, the shoes, the long gloves, if that's what you plan to wear. You will get the clearest picture of which dress is best for you and whether everything fits comfortably together.

While it's fine to start shopping for the dress as early as a year before your celebration, you do not want to have your final fitting any sooner than three or four months before the celebration. Starting early will give the dress shop plenty of time to order the dresses, especially for the court of honor, and will give the seamstress enough time to make all the damas' dresses and their accessories.

A Dress Shop or a Dressmaker?

Latino bridal shops are a treasure trove of quinceañera dresses. After culling through the bridal magazines and talking with their friends, most girls and their mothers turn to a dress shop to see what is out there, to see if their dream dress is ready made.

Benita Arevalo, however, went to a dress shop to avoid the temptation of constantly changing details on a dress made by a seamstress in an attempt to make it perfect. "I knew surely, some way, somehow, it wouldn't come out exactly the way I wanted it," she said. "So I just decided to buy it. So my mom wouldn't have to go crazy with me going back and changing things." Benita wanted a pale pink dress, and the shop took care of getting it dyed to the right shade.

§ § The World's Only Designer Discount Outlet § §

Going to be in South Florida? Check out Alfred Angelo Dreammaker's outlet in the Sawgrass Mills Mall in Sunrise. Time your visit right, and you can find satin dresses for as low as $109, tulle for $139.

Normally, you will save 75 percent off the retail price of an Alfred Angelo Dreammaker dress. In a bridal shop, these dresses start at around $460. Then again, the outlet offers no alterations.

In addition to the dresses, which are discontinued models from the previous season, the shop offers slips, shoes, shoe clips, and headpieces.

Sometimes girls have two dresses designed in one. Fanny Padilla wore this floor length gown for church. For the dance, she removed the detachable long hooped skirt, leaving a chic short dress. —Pilsen Photo Studio

But often trying on dresses off the rack brings out the designer in everyone. "When you buy a dress already made, and then you want the sleeves a certain way, it's going to cost you more to take that dress apart than it is to have it made," said Rita Aguirre. That's when you turn to the dressmaker.

The dressmaker can give you countless options and make a dress that is uniquely you. You may start with the seed of an idea from a picture in a magazine. Soon-to-be quinceañeras walk into the Fiesta Azteca dress shop with magazines in hand, said the owner, Maria Ramos. "I make the dresses from the pictures. I chose the material, or they say I want it in this material, this skirt with that bodice, with the sleeves from a third. They tell me what they want and I make it." The fabric and the amount of work determine how much the seamstress charges.

The first price a dress shop or seamstress offers you is not necessarily the best price. Sarah Arevalo paid cash for the dress she bought for her daughter Benita and saved 15 percent off the tag price.

Dressmakers will shave some savings for the customer from the price they first quote for a quinceañera dress, but the more you buy, the bigger the discount. You will save more if the same seamstress also makes the court's dresses, their headpieces and if you are using silk flowers, their wrist corsages or hand bouquets as well. She may shave off still more if you have her make at least some of the decorations and the capias as well (see p. 186).

On the Mexican side of the Texas-Mexico border, you can have a dress made within days for around $80, an entire package that includes the crown for $115.

A Labor of Love

In Puerto Rico, someone in the family who knows how to sew often makes the quinceañera's dress as their gift to her, said Norma Garcia, the director of the Campos Albizu Community Center in New York City. The quinceañera's dress is traditionally white, Garcia said, trimmed with the color worn by the damas. "Usually it's very pastel colors, very subtle colors," said Garcia, who threw a celebration for her daughter at the Roosevelt Hotel in 1988.

Whether you celebrate in a hotel or at home, the long white dress was what you wore, said Gloria Bernabe-Ramos, a professor at the University of Massachusetts at Amherst. The dresses were very special, often embroidered by hand. "It was a big thing."

❧ ❧ *Rentals—A Smart Alternative* ❧ ❧

Want a drop-dead designer dress for a fraction of what it would cost to buy? Try a shop that specializes in dress rentals. If you are not sentimental about keeping your dress, renting can be a cost-saving alternative for you and your court.

Esthersita Nodarse, a party planner who has organized quinceañeras in the Miami area for more than two decades, advocates renting to her clients. "A new dress will cost between $2,000 and $5,000," said Nodarse. "If they rent it, it costs between $800 and $1,200."

When you rent, you pick up the dress a day or two before your celebration and return it a day or two after. Most places require a contract, which not only states the days of pickup and return, but that you are liable for any permanent damage—rips, tears, and indelible stains. Most rental companies also require a deposit. You can find them in the yellow pages.

This side of the Rio Grande, however, the going rate starts at $250 and goes straight to the multi-thousand-dollar stratosphere. The average dress runs around $500.

While dressmakers advertise in newspapers, and many party planners and banquet hall managers can recommend people, most quinceañeras find their dressmakers through friends and family. Many work out of their homes.

Michael Eid, who manages Naomi's Bridal and Formal Wear II in Fort Lauderdale, Florida, advises girls not to get their dresses earlier than four months before their celebration, to make sure it fits. "It takes two months to order the dress, one month for alterations, and one month for security," said Eid.

Choosing a Color

White? Or pink? There are two philosophies when it comes to what color the quinceañera should wear. Some people say white, the symbol of purity, is the only color for a quinceañera. Others say white is for weddings; a quinceañera should wear pink or another pastel. Still others compromise by trimming a white dress with the theme color, sported by the court.

"The colors change from year to year," said Concepción Aguilar. "Some years, peach is very popular. Last year, 1995, many girls used pink, and there have been times when they used a lot of lilac or aqua."

The colors that quinceañeras in Chicago use are strong—red, maroon, and purple.

Puerto Rican and Dominican quinceañeras sometimes have a rainbow court. The girls all wear the same style dresses, but the colors are different pastels. The girls who have the closest relationship with the quinceañera, such as a sister, choose the color they want to wear first, then cousins get to pick, then friends.

The All-Important Dress

Cinderella's ball gown is often copied by quinceañeras, but next to their dresses it looks positively plain. They're made of iridescent ruffles and gossamer bows, shimmering satins and taffeta, clouds of tulle, glittering sequins and pearls on embroidered lace. They are fashion confections, the stuff of dreams. The skirt may be hooped or simply buoyed with crinolines. But they are all long and feminine, and should have an air of innocence.

"You need to be as conservative as possible," said Sarah Arevalo, who organized quinceañeras for both her daughters. The girls, however, want to wear something more daring, more revealing, more, well, womanly. Dresses with bare backs and low necklines are appealing, but not really appropriate. Your dressmaker can help create the illusion of what you want while giving your mother what she wants to see on you—coverage.

Keep in mind that you will not only be stand-

Honoring a Memory

Fanny Padilla of Chicago likes red and white, which is why she picked them as theme colors for her quinceañera in 1995. But she had another reason to pick them. Her grandfather, who died in her native Honduras three years earlier, had been active in the Liberal Party. Its colors are red and white.

ing and posing for pictures the day of your celebration. Much of the time, you will be dancing. "When people pick out their dresses, they think about the photographs or the video, but they don't think about the music they'll be dancing to," said Andres Trujillo, a violinist who plays duets in the Miami area with his wife, Darlene, as well as with an orchestra, Almendra. "A dress that's beautiful for the waltz or for a bolero won't work as well when you're dancing a merengue or the Macarena. If you want a lot of different music styles, you have to think about what you're wearing, or choose a dress that will change or that lets you move."

The quinceañera wears her dress from the time she steps into the church in the afternoon until she twirls for the last time on the dance floor. That is tradition. But fashion is beginning to bend the rules, and some girls are having dresses made so

Tradition vs. Tradition

Laura Valenzuela had been steeped in cultural tradition since the age of five, when she followed her older sister into the Mexican Folkloric Dance Company of Chicago. So when it came time to decide what she would wear for her quinceañera, she wavered between a traditional ball gown and a *china poblana*—a traditional "peasant" skirt and blouse richly embroidered with sequins and spangles. "I had never worn one before," said Laura. "I wanted just to wear it, just to remind people." Back and forth Laura wavered between the two styles, until she finally decided to wear a white ball gown. But at her reception, as she waited for her party to start, her mother gave her a special present—a white satin dress edged with green and red ribbon. Across the skirt was embroidered Mexico's national symbol: the spangled serpent gleamed in the glittering eagle's mouth. As part of her choreography to celebrate her coming of age, Laura danced in her very own *china poblana*.

the long full skirt is removable and a shorter party dress remains. "Sometimes I attach a short skirt to the bodice, then the overskirt unbuttons and comes off," said Concepción Aguilar. "The juncture is covered with decoration. When they finish dancing the waltz, she takes off the skirt of the dress."

Among Hondurans, the quinceañera dress is customarily made with a removable overskirt, said María Lourdes García de Padilla, Fanny's mother. After the waltz, after the shoes are changed from flats to heels, the quinceañera takes off the wide, full skirt, and a more narrow skirt remains.

Laura Valenzuela also had two dresses in one. Underneath the long full coatdress she wore for the mass, Laura had a short slim dress, which she wore for the dance just by removing the outer layer after the waltz. Laura's mother, Ana Maria Valenzuela, advises people to get a rough sketch of the dress you have discussed with the dressmaker, so you can think about it later at home.

The Headpieces: The Tocado and Crown

How many headpieces you will need and what they are made of is up to you, your family, and the traditions of your culture.

If you are planning on having a church service or will be crowned with a tiara during your presentation at the reception, you'll need at least two. Benita Arevalo, who had a Tejano theme, had not one but *three* headpieces. For her mass, she wore a pearl crown. She marched into the reception wearing a white Tejano hat decorated with tulle and pink flowers, and her madrina crowned her with rhinestones for her presentation.

The headpiece you wear in church may be a comb decorated with flowers designed to tuck into your hair on the side or it may be like the one Liliana Alvarez wore at her quinceañera in 1988 in Texas. Liliana's birthday is on Valentine's Day, and her colors were red and white. At mass, a wreath of white and red silk flowers encircled her head, and white and red ribbons decorated the back of the headpiece.

Many Puerto Rican quinceañeras have crowns of orange blossoms (a symbol of purity) or another kind of fresh or silk flower, as well as the rhinestone tiara, said Enit Negrón, a Chicago hairdresser who has many quinceañera clients and who had one for her daughter, Millie.

Many quinceañeras in Chicago also wear floral wreaths at mass, said Concepción Aguilar, which the girl's parents buy. The madrina de la corona buys the rhinestone crown, takes it to the hall or wherever the reception is being held, and places it on the quinceañera during the presentation.

Blanca Argueta, whose family is Salvadoran, did not have a mass. She entered her party bareheaded and then was crowned with a rhinestone tiara as part of her presentation.

In Honduras, however, the only daughter or the youngest daughter wears a rhinestone tiara. Fanny Padilla, the oldest of four girls in her family, wore a pearl headpiece throughout the mass and reception, in keeping with her cultural tradition.

When Celia Hernandez stepped onto the sidewalk in front of San Antonio's San Fernando cathedral, she looked like a madonna. A pink mantilla that matched the color of her dress covered her head and fell to the first ruffle at her hem. At the reception she wore a pearl and ribbon headpiece, which the madrina de la corona replaced during her presentation with a rhinestone tiara.

Other Accessories

Many quinceañeras also wear lace gloves or mitts (fingerless gloves) that match the dress's color. If the sleeves on the dress are short, they may wear long, elegant eighteen-button gloves.

If changing the shoes is part of the way your culture celebrates your attaining quince años, you will also need a pair of flats and a pair of heels. There is no correlation between the height of your heels and how grown up people think you are. Rather, they will think you are more mature if you buy shoes you will be able to wear throughout the night. A mid-heel pump, two to three inches high, will keep you dancing all night, rather than a four- or five-inch strappy sandal, which you will want to abandon after the first cumbia. The idea is to kick up your heels, not kick them off.

Be sure to take all your accessories with you to your last fitting, including your shoes and the undergarments you will be wearing with your dress. It will help the seamstress give you the best possible fit and give you a good idea of how beautiful you will look for your very special day.

Capias and the Capia Doll

Capias are the printed ribbon favors that commemorate the party. Each carries out the theme in the color and style of the celebration. The ribbon has the quinceañera's name and the date of the party. The capia doll is a miniature version of the birthday girl herself, eternally captured as the quinceañera.

"They cover the whole doll with capias, and what's left [after they're distributed] is the quinceañera," said Concepción Aguilar. "The dress is a copy of hers." If you're having padrinos, the doll and capias are the contribution of la madrina de las capias.

The dressmaker often makes the doll's dress from the scraps of material and trim left over from the quinceañera's dress. Sometimes she makes the capias as well.

Dressing the Court of Honor

THE DAMAS

If everyone in the court looked like Daisy Fuentes, picking their dresses would be easy. But they're not. Some are short and plump, others tall and willowy. The trick is to find a style that all the damas can live with, one that makes them feel beautiful and that they can afford.

Once you have an idea of what you would like your damas to wear, take a sketch or picture to them or accompany them to the dress shop. Can they wear it? Is it cut too low? Too tight? Will their parents approve of the style and price? Do not forget the hairpiece and the bouquet or wrist corsage.

Benita Arevalo decided to avoid the issue of the dresses for her court altogether. By choosing a Tejano theme, she dressed everyone, boys and girls alike, in black boots, jeans, and tuxedo shirts. The pink cummerbunds and bow ties each wore echoed the pink and white color theme Benita had chosen. Everyone wore cowboy hats, but the girls' hats were decorated with white tulle and pink ribbons. Each girl carried a pink silk rose adorned with pink and white ribbons, too.

The dama de honor, the honor attendant, may wear a dress that's a bit different from the rest of the court. All the damas in Celia Hernandez's court wore the same style dress, but the color distinguished Veronica Sanchez as the dama de honor. While the other damas wore solid maroon, the bodice on Veronica's dress was pink.

THE CHAMBELANES

Because boys often wear tuxedos to a quinceañera, all they have to do is give their measurements and money to the people at the formal-wear store or to the quinceañera's mother. Then they're done until the day of the party, right?

Not quite.

More things can go wrong with a tuxedo than you could ever imagine. Each boy should pick up his tuxedo as soon as it comes in. They should make sure they have what they are supposed to in the right size, preferably before they leave the store. If they are supposed to have studs—the metal clasps that formal shirts sometimes have instead of buttons—they should check to see if they are all there. Is the shirt the right style? How about the vest—is it there? Is it the right style, fabric, and color? If they are wearing a bow tie and cummerbund, are these the right color and size? Waiting until the last minute to check such things leaves no leeway to correct errors.

If your celebration is less formal you can save the chambelanes the rental expense by having them wear something more casual or culturally traditional. If your heritage is Caribbean, for example, you might choose long-sleeved white guayaberas, the traditional man's shirt with the tucks down the front. A simple but elegant look could be a plain white shirts, dark trousers, and cummerbunds that match the color of the damas' dresses.

Queen for a Day

Toward the end of the 1970s and the beginning of the 1980s, the quinceañera in Chicago was more than a princess. She was queen for a day. Besides her gown, the quinceañera wore a velvet cape. She not only wore a rhinestone crown but held a scepter in her hand. Quinceañeras in Philadelphia wore capes into the late 1980s. As the eighties became the nineties, the queen changed into a princess and she ceased to wear her royal trappings. Well, some of them, anyway.

THE PRINCE AND PRINCESS

The princess is often the flower girl, the one who carries a basket of petals and strews them in the quinceañera's path as she enters and leaves the church. Her escort, the prince, carries the cushion for the quinceañera to kneel on at the church service. Their clothes will be slightly different from the older members of the court, something more appropriate for a young child, but their attire should be coordinated.

THE SYMBOL OF INNOCENCE

At Central American celebrations, a very special member of the court is the symbol of innocence. She is usually no older than seven or eight and often younger, and is dressed identically to the quinceañera. At Jacqueline Delao's celebration, her toddler niece, Lissette Schener, had the honor. Like Jackie, she wore a white dress with gold brocade trim, styled after Cinderella's ball gown, and wore a tiny tiara.

THE QUINCEAÑERA'S PARENTS

Blanca Argueta's dad wore a white tie and cutaway coat for her quinceañera in Bay Shore, New York, as did Teresa Perez's father in Hialeah. How you want your father dressed depends on how formal your celebration is. If he objects to wearing a tuxedo, a dark suit is also appropriate, as is a long-sleeved white guayabera. You may also want to honor your grandfather and baptismal godfather, even if their only role is to help you celebrate, by asking them to wear tuxedos, dark suits, or guayaberas, too.

For your mother, grandmother, and baptismal godmother, your celebration is a great reason for them to dress as fancy as they want to be and you want them to. Beaded dresses, satins, and silks are all appropriate and will make your celebration look even more elegant. They may want to go the extra step and find dresses in your theme colors.

In Chicago, the padrinos de velación, the ones who sponsor the church, often wear the same color as the court, but the madrina wears a different style dress. The padrino may wear a tie of the same color.

Hair and Makeup: Finishing Touches

Whether you wear your hair long and flowing or swept up in a sophisticated chignon or twist, it has to work with the headpiece. Often there is someone in the family with a talent for hair and makeup, but if not, or you want to have professional attention, make your appointments at least four months in advance. That way you will get the dates you want. Set a separate appointment for the initial consultation, any photo shoots that are scheduled, and the day of the celebration itself. A consultation appointment early on will give the hairdresser a chance to find out what you have in mind and create a hairstyle that you like and that works for you. Look through your favorite magazines to get ideas for hairstyles, and keep the pictures you cut out tucked in your notebook of dreams to show your hairdresser when you have your appointment.

If you would like your hairdresser to fix the damas' hair as well, talk with him or her about the logistics. You may decide to have the hairdresser come to you. If so, they will charge by the hour or the day. This can work especially well if the damas are all coming to dress at your house beforehand. But be honest about the number of people he or she will have to accommodate. A less-than-accurate number will only frustrate everyone and make you late.

If you decide to consult a makeup artist, do so several months before your celebration. When you go for your appointment, write down everything he or she does, including the products and shade used and how the makeup was applied. That way you can duplicate what she does on your big day.

Make sure you have the right color lipstick, and if you are doing your nails, nail polish on hand, either to take to the manicurist the day before the celebration or to do your hands yourself.

With your dress ready, your hair styled, and your makeup on, you are ready for the trial run—your formal portrait.

Chapter Ten ∾

Smile for the Cameras!: Photographers and Videographers

There are no two fifteens alike, because they all do something different.

—*Tony Rodriguez, Twins Video, Miami*

Nearly forty years later, Gloria Rodriguez still likes looking at her sister's quinceañera pictures. "They were taken at a studio," said Rodriguez, who heads the nationally renowned child development program Avance. "That's the way it was done in those days. You went to the studio and had formal pictures taken."

More recently, Abraham Ganz slides the black cassette into the VCR at his home on Long Island, New York, and relives the magic night that his daughter, Debbie, came of age. "It's a night you'll always remember," he told *Newsday* in a 1987 article.

Quinceañeras are the stuff of memories. But when the memory grows dim, the pictures carefully kept in a photo album and the video recording of the festivities preserve every precious detail. You'll need to find a photographer and videographer you trust to capture all those precious moments the way you want them recalled. It's easy to confuse quantity with quality when you begin looking at video packages.

FACING PAGE: *Outdoor locations are often chosen for the formal quinceañera portrait. Teresita Perez chose one of Miami's beautiful gardens.* —Panorama Photo Studio and Video Productions

The photographer and the videographer you choose should have experience shooting a quinceañera. If you have to spend your time explaining the ceremony and the customs, you'll have less time to spend with your guests and more stress. And you run the chance of someone not familiar with the celebration missing an important part, simply because he or she did not recognize its importance.

Some churches can be strict about photographing or taping the ceremony; check with them before you begin your search to see what their requirements are. Some churches will permit only their own videographers to tape quinces services. You can choose whomever you want for the reception, but for the church ceremony, you have to use theirs at whatever their rate is.

The still photographer sets his or her rate by the number and size of the photos you want. Some packages include formal and semiformal portraits shot in the studio several months before the celebration; some include only pictures taken at the church and reception. The videographer charges for the number of cameras used to shoot the celebration for the title sequence—whether it's static or animated—and sometimes for an opening montage of photographs, which you supply. With both media, the extra time you take to think about the shots you want and how many photos you will need will make shopping for the professionals easier and help them give you what you want.

What Images Do I Want to Capture?

Before you actually start looking for a photographer or videographer, take the time to think about the specific images through which you'll want to remember your quinceañera. Is your grandmother bringing your dress from the Dominican Republic? Then you may want a shot of the two of you as she is helping you get ready. What about one with your baby sister? Or one of your mother dancing at the reception with her brother, Tío Alfonso, whom she has not seen since she left El Salvador ten years ago? Do you want photographs of the people seated at each table? Do you want the photographer to bring his equipment to the reception to shoot formal portraits of you with your guests?

For Your Photos

Think about the shots you want the photographer to take and make a list that becomes part of the contract. You will have plenty to think of on the day of the celebration without trying to remember what images you want the photographer to capture. And having a list helps him or her plan how to take those shots as well.

Before you get to the photographer's studio, consider the following questions, which will help you select the right package.

- Do you want an 18-by-20-inch framed formal portrait to stand in the hallway when the guests arrive? Will you need a smaller print of that portrait for the printer to duplicate on your invitations? What about a series of informal studio shots?
- Do you want to tuck wallet-sized photos into the thank-you notes?
- Were you planning to give each member of the court a 5-by-7-inch photo as a way of thanking them for being there for you? Do you want each set of grandparents to have a complete album, or will an 8-by-10-inch portrait do? If your parents are divorced or separated, will you need two full albums? If you are on a budget, you may want just a formal portrait of you in your dress, taken at the studio. That could run you less than $100.

For Your Video

Planning what photographs you want taken is as simple as making a list. For your videotape, however, you may want to think about how you will want the finished tape to look:

- Do you want to include a collage of photographs that start with your baby pictures and show you growing up?
- Are there specific segments you want taped and edited in a specific order?
- Do you want animated titles?
- Is there special music or a song you want for the opening and closing?

Telling the photographer and videographer what the most important elements of your celebration are ensures that you will remember your quinceañera the way you want to, highlighting your favorite parts. Make a list so you can discuss what you want with the photographer and videographer. That way he or she can tell you what's possible and what isn't. At the same time, he or she knows specifically what to shoot, how to shoot it, and how to edit the tape to your liking or which shots to proof so you can select the best photos for your album. Be as specific as you can about what you want emphasized on camera. Frank and Tony Rodriguez, identical twins who specialize in two-camera videos for social events, once did a tape for a quinceañera who wanted the cake highlighted because she and her mother had made it themselves. "They were so crazy about that cake," Frank recalled. "They said, 'We want you to tape the salon empty, getting all the detail, but mainly the cake, please. Go slow with the cake.' So we showed every single detail of that cake from every angle."

Choosing a Photographer

The photographer's schedule fills up fast. You should start looking at albums and studios six to nine months before your celebration. Meet with several, so you know who you are most comfortable with, whose work you like best, and who is offering you the best deal.

You may want to start the conversation with a photographer by asking to see the price list. But determining whether you like his or her work is just as important. Ask to see several albums of quinceañeras that the photographer has shot recently. If you are dealing with a large studio or one that uses several photographers, ask to see sample albums showing each one's work.

Be sure to ask the photographer you consult whether he or she is going to be the one doing the actual shooting. If the photographer makes multiple commitments and customarily subcontracts out some of the work, you want to know that up front. That's why it's important to see the work of each photographer at a studio.

Photographers generally sell their services in packages that vary by the number of shots and the size of the photographs. Packages can run from $200 for a few studio

In this picture, taken in 1956, Maria Antonia Reyes holds her prayer book and rosary in one gloved hand. The bolero jacket and matching beret were worn with the tea-length dress to mass, and the afternoon party held in her parents' San Antonio home, in keeping with tradition at the time. —Courtesy of the Reyes family

portraits and a small album shot at the church or reception to several thousand dollars for formal studio portraits, location shots at a fancy hotel lobby or in a park, and photos taken throughout the day of the celebration. Take the list of shots you want included in an album and try to match what you want with what the photographer offers. Think about how you will use the photos in the package and ask if substitutions can be made.

If your budget is tight, ask about getting one or two studio portraits of you in your gown, or ordering a small package and asking the photographer to shoot either the church service or the presentation and choreography at the reception. But instead of sending photos to your guests, put a disposable camera on each table. That way the guests can take what shots they like of the reception and can take the camera home to have the pictures developed themselves.

Choosing a Videographer

There are two things people want to know quickly about a videographer: the price and whether the date they want is open. But quality is an element that should not be over-looked.

When you meet with the videographer, ask to see a finished tape from a quinceañera he or she has shot recently, preferably one held in the same place you are having yours. Try to see as many different videos from as many different videographers as you can. "Once you see four or five or six different videographers, they already have an idea what a quinceañera video is and what they would like," says Frank Rodriguez. Be sure to ask the videographer whether he or she has taped a quinceañera at the place where your event will be held. Ask to see that video so you can get an idea of how yours will look.

Tony Rodriguez likens editing a video to decorating a cake. "When you pull it out of the oven, what does it look like? Nothing. Then when they put on the frosting and the flowers and the this and that, you say, 'Wow! It looks beautiful.' In video it's the same thing—the raw material that you just shot with a camera, if you view it like that, you get bored. But once you start doing the titles, the editing, the sound, the mixing, the effects, you say, 'Wow! It looks nice!' "

During the consultation, the twins show the quinceañera and her family a video that's close to their plans. They ask them what they liked and did not like about the video, what they would like done differently. The twins emphasize that, unlike a movie, a quinceañera is real life. "In a movie, if something doesn't come out right, you say, 'Cut. Do it again.' But with a video, you can't stop a choreography because there's something wrong with the camera. That's why you need to see how they handle those situations."

By analyzing the video segment by segment, you will get an idea of what is possible in the editing. The twins specialize in two-camera videos, not only because there are two of them, but also because using two cameras gives them more options when it's time to edit the tape. People are used to watching multicamera productions on television, and two cameras allow the videographer to come closer to that standard.

The Contract

The contract is the blueprint you and the photographer or videographer share to capture your memories on film or tape. It outlines their obligations to you and your obligations to them. Be as clear as you can about what you want. That's what a contract is for—to specify what you want in writing and what is being offered you for your money. Most professionals will welcome your specificity and will have plenty of items of their own to include. But if the videographer or photographer gets upset if you want specifics in writing, resume your search, no matter how comfortable you are with him or her.

When you are ready to sign the contract, your deposit is due, generally a third to a half the total cost of the package. The rest is due before the day of the quinceañera. Too many photographers and videographers have done the work of shooting and proofing the film or editing the tape, only to have the people never pick up their albums or tapes. Before signing any contract, be sure to read it carefully and make sure you understand everything. These are the things it should include:

- The dates, times, and places the photographer or videographer is to take pictures.
- Who the individual photographer or videographer will be, *not just the company.*

❧ ❧ *What to Look for in a Photographer and Videographer* ❧ ❧

- Does he or she have a good reputation? How long have they been in business?
  Do they have experience shooting quinceañeras?

- Can he or she control people and be pleasant at the same time?

- What equipment does he or she use? What happens if something breaks?

- How many events a day does he or she schedule? Shooting several events the same
  day is not a problem, but there should be at least a couple of hours between jobs.

- Will the photographer with whom you discussed your plans be the one who will
  actually shoot your celebration? Or will the studio send someone else?

- If you want a location shot, is there a site fee? Is it included in the package?

- Both the quality of the product and the quality of the service should be excellent.

FOR PHOTOGRAPHERS

- What kind of film and paper does he or she use to print the photos?
  Who processes and prints the pictures?

- How are the negatives stored? They should be dated and filed at the studio.
  How long does the photographer keep them?

FOR VIDEOGRAPHERS

- What kind of sound equipment does the videographer use? Is the priest miked?
  The music in the church? The MC at the reception?

- What sources are there for the sound? Does the videographer use an equalizer
  to edit the sound, to boost the voice if needed? What is the source for the
  music track, if you are using one? Are special effects available?

- What kind of tape does the videographer use? What kind of tape is used for the
  cassette? VHS has 240 lines of resolution, while super VHS, or SVHS, has 400.
  The more lines of resolution, the clearer the picture. But SVHS will play only on an
  SVHS-capable recorder and a high-resolution monitor. Make sure the cassette you are
  getting is compatible with the equipment you have.

- Does the videographer maintain a library of the edited tapes?

- How long the shooter will be at the event; whether you are paying to have his or her services for a certain number of hours or for the duration of the celebration. If the agreement is for a set number of hours, find out the overtime rate and have it specified in the contract.
- The price and the terms of payment: how much was put down on deposit at signing and when the balance is due. Specify under what terms the deposit is refundable.
- Any specific shots, music, editing of the videotape.
- The number and size of photos; the length and number of videocassettes.
- The date the video or albums will be delivered.
- Anything else you feel is important to specify in writing.

Scheduling Your Formal Portrait

In some parts of the country, all the photographs are taken the day of the celebration. The quinceañera, her court, and her family go to the studio between the church service and the reception to have the formal portraits taken. Generally, pictures of the individual court members are taken, then pictures of each couple. The quinceañera with her full court is taken, and then the family portraits, culminating with the pictures of the quinceañera alone.

In other parts of the country, however, formal and informal portraits are taken several months before the celebration. Either or both can be used on the invitation and matted and displayed at the entrance of the party. Often the guests sign the mat surrounding the picture, instead of a guest book, with their good wishes for the honoree.

For the portrait, "the girl comes to the studio in her dress—or it can be in plain clothes, something sporty, but nice," said Juan Muñoz. Sometimes the portraits are shot on location, in a beautiful hotel lobby or a park with lush greenery or a waterfront. Sometimes places charge a site fee. Check with the photographer to see if the site fee is included in the package.

Hair and makeup appointments for the studio portraits should be made well in advance, to allow you to get to the studio on time. Be sure to arrive promptly.

Chapter Eleven ❧

Start Spreading the News:
The Invitations and Announcements

Tengo el gusto de invitarles
a la celebración de mis Quince Años
que me ofrecerán mis padres . . .

—La invitación de Teresita Perez

I have the pleasure of inviting you
to the celebration of my Fifteenth Birthday
that my parents will have for me . . .

—a translation of Teresita Perez's invitation

Graciela Alfaro checked and double-checked the guest list to make sure she had forgotten no one she wanted to invite to the quinceañera of her oldest daughter, Lisa. A month before the celebration, the white envelopes arrived at three hundred homes across the country. A white invitation slid from the shiny purple lining. On the front, a young girl in a ruffled dress, surrounded by roses, daisies, and tiny hearts, held two doves in her outstretched hand. The entire scene was embossed in pearlized white ink, including the words *Quince Años*—fifteen years.

Three months earlier, Graciela Alfaro had ordered the invitations directly from a local printer. The purple lining and the matching purple ink used to print the invitations

FACING PAGE: *The invitation your guests receive is their first glimpse of the festivities you have planned for your celebration.* —Richard Haro

echoed the color theme—purple and white—calling Lisa's family and friends to Chicago to celebrate her milestone birthday.

Your invitations are the first glimpse your guests have of your upcoming celebration. There are many elements to consider—from the number you need to their design, from the wording to what, exactly, you are paying for. Order the invitations with plenty of time to spare, just in case they have to be redone. Four months gives you a comfortable cushion, although some mail-order invitation companies can have your order printed and shipped within forty-eight hours.

Be sure to proofread your order as soon as it arrives. If you are listing the names of the court and the padrinos in the invitation, make sure that everyone listed is in fact participating and that their names are spelled correctly.

Invitations should be delivered at least three weeks and mailed at least six weeks before the celebration, especially if they are going to guests who are out of the country.

Family and friends have talked about the upcoming celebration and helped you plan for months. Now is the time to finalize the guest list as the first step in ordering the invitations.

Finalizing the Guest List

Some say the strongest reason for keeping the quinceañera tradition is that it brings families together to make happy memories. For the aunts and uncles and cousins who live in the States but we do not often get to see, for the grandparents who are still in our home countries, the quinceañera is a perfect occasion to bring everyone together to celebrate the coming of age of one of their niñas.

When quinceañera celebrations were held at home, everyone in the family was invited. In the Rio Grande Valley of Texas, where quinceañeras are held on the family ranch as often as they are held at a hotel ballroom, hundreds of people may attend, and celebrations attended by a thousand or more guests—most of them family or friends of family—are not unheard of. As we settle into cities and hold our celebrations at country clubs and banquet halls, our celebrations are smaller—averaging between two and five hundred guests—but no less heartfelt.

And not just *your* family is asked to come. The families of the court of honor, the families of the padrinos, sometimes even the families of the professionals who made the celebration possible—the dressmaker, the hairdresser, the caterer, the choreographer—are invited as well.

"It's not just geared for the quinceañeras, it's for family," said Norma Garcia, recalling the traditions in Puerto Rico. "Over here the teenagers come alone. Over there if you invite your girlfriend, the girlfriend will bring her parents. And if it's a boy, he will bring his parents. And you arrange the tables by family. And that's the way it should be."

More than six months before the party, Maria Magaña and her mother, Leticia, were wrangling over who was to be on the guest list and who was not. Leticia Magaña wanted to limit the friends Maria invited to those whose families Leticia knows. Maria wanted to invite friends from school, regardless of whether her mother knew them, let alone their families. For Leticia Magaña, keeping tight control of the guest list is as much a security issue as an economic one. At some celebrations, gang fights have broken out, including one in 1995 at a fashionable Central Park West church hall in New York City where at least one person died in a hail of gunfire.

But apart from the security issue is economics. If you are making the food yourself, you can stretch here and there to accommodate unexpected guests. Caterers, however, charge per plate, regardless of whether that plate is served to an adult or to a child. At the $20 and up per plate that a caterer charges, the unexpected thirty-five people who turned up at a celebration in Hialeah, Florida, can mean an extra $700 on the bill.

Although we love our children dearly, sometimes it is just not possible to invite the very young children of our guests. To stay within budget, sometimes the guest list is limited to people over twelve or thirteen years old; sometimes only the children of the immediate family are invited, regardless of age. Other times the invitation or reception card will simply say "No Niños."

When it's time to look for places to pare down the guest list, adults and teens are given priority over children. Whether the girlfriend or boyfriend of a single member of a family is invited depends on how long they have been going out together, how serious the relationship is, and how close you are to your maximum catering number.

The members of the court of honor and the padrinos are usually allowed to bring additional members of their family or friends, as a way of thanking them for the months of practice and the expense of participating. For less formal fiestas, the mother of the quinceañera simply calls the guest and asks how many reception cards they will need to include in the invitation, or if the invitations are delivered by hand, how many they will need for their guests. For more formal fiestas, however, they will ask the guest for their guests' name and address, and send an invitation to them directly.

Your notebook is the perfect place to keep track of the guest list. Think of the people who are closest to you, that you want most of all to be with you to celebrate your special day. Their names should go near the top. Next are the members of the court and their families, the padrinos, if you are having them, and their families, your friends and their parents, the party professionals who helped you make this dream come true, and their families. Be sure to include the name, address, and telephone number for each guest. Leave enough space so you can jot down whether they will be attending and the number of people who will be in their party. That way, all the information is in one handy place and you will have a good idea of the number of people planning to attend.

If the quinceañera plans to invite her friends, talk about a number to invite that is acceptable to mother and daughter alike. Or invite the friends to the dance alone. If security is a concern, however, make sure that the friends you want to come present invitations at the door.

The guest list not only gives you a count of how many guests to prepare for but also of how many invitations to have printed. And no matter what the count of the guest list, you will need an extra twenty-five to fifty to send to out-of-town family who might not be likely to come, but will surely be pleased when they pull the invitation from the envelope and realize the important milestone you've reached.

What Stationery to Order

Most people turn to bridal shops and printers when it's time to order the invitations. Depending on your budget, how formal your celebration is, and whether you are inviting all your guests to all parts of the celebration, these are some of the items you may want to order. All you really need are the invitations to the celebration itself. All the other items are nice touches, but are by no means a must.

- **Invitations to the court of honor.** Asks friends and family to participate in your court.
- **Invitations to the celebration.** Sets the theme and color scheme of your party and asks people to come celebrate your important day.
- **Reception card.** Tells the guests when and where the reception is to be held. By asking people to present the reception card at the door, you ensure that those who were invited are those who attend. Nivaldo Cruz, president of Angelito's Banquet Hall in Hialeah, Florida, recommends the cards also be engraved or thermographed in the theme color, along with the invitations, in order to prevent forgeries.
- **Reply card and envelopes.** Encourages a prompt reply to your invitation. However, you must address and put postage on the envelopes and make sure the envelopes are large enough for the post office to deliver.
- **Pew card.** If you're having a church service and you want the first few rows reserved for immediate family members and padrinos, mail these, one per person, after the invitation is accepted.
- **List of members of the court of honor and padrinos.** Usually printed on onionskin or tissue paper and inserted into the invitation, if the names have not been printed on the invitation itself.
- **Inner envelope.** If you have any inserts, this holds the whole package together. When the invitation is inserted, the side with the fold goes in first. If there is no fold, the invitation is inserted so it is upright when slid out. On the outside of the inner envelope, the title and surname of those who are invited are written. For example: Sr. y

Sra. Chavez on the first line; Daniela Chavez, Carlos Chavez, y Jane Chavez (their teenage children) on the second, third, and fourth lines. The inner envelope is not sealed before it is inserted into the outer envelope, flap to the back, so the name faces the guest.

- **Outer envelope.** This is the wrapper that enables the post office to deliver all the elements at once. On the most formal invitations, the only words that may be abbreviated are Mr., Mrs., Ms., Dr., Sr., Sra., and Srta. Everything else, including "street," "avenue," and the names of the states should be spelled out. The return address is written in the envelope's upper right-hand corner.

In addition, you may also want to order:

- **Thank-you scrolls to be given at the reception.** These are messages printed on strips of textured paper, rolled into scrolls, and often tied with ribbon and secured with tiny bows and roses. The quinceañera gives one to each guest when she pins the capias on everyone at the reception, or they can be left at each dinner setting or given out as each guest leaves.
- **Thank-you notes for the guests.** Instead of the scrolls at the reception, you may prefer to mail thank-you notes to your guests for attending your party. Teresa Perez sent thank-you notes to everyone who came to her quinces.

Gracias por haber compartido
conmigo la celebración de mis
Quince Años
Fué la presencia de ustedes
la que hizo de esta fiesta
un recuerdo el cual
siempre vivirá en mi corazón
Con todo cariño
Teresita

Thank you for having shared
with me the celebration of my
Fifteenth Birthday
It was your presence
that made this celebration
a memory that
will always live in my heart
With affection
Teresita

- **Informal note cards for thank-you notes for gifts.** Informal note cards, which are blank inside but printed with the name of the quinceañera on the front, can be used for penning thank-you notes to guests who brought gifts and padrinos. If you choose to have a thank-you message printed inside, be sure to include a short personalized note of thanks as well.
- **Napkins.** These napkins are most often served with the cake and may be printed with the quinceañera's theme, in her colors, or with her picture, as well as her name and the date of the celebration.
- **Place Cards.** These cards are between 3 and 4 inches high and 3¾ and 5 inches wide. They tell guests at which table you have seated them or which place at the table is theirs, depending on the system you are using. You can order them from the printer with an emblem of the theme, but check with the caterer or reception site manager to see if they are provided as part of the service.
- **Programs.** If you are having a church service, you may want to have a program printed for your guests. Sometimes this is included with the church fee. For Carolina Vasquez's Mass of Thanksgiving, the Reverend Susan Birkelo, the pastor of Iglesia Luterana La Trinidad in Chicago, had an eighteen-page bilingual program printed of the entire service, including hymns, so that people could lift their voices in prayer and song.

Lisa Alfaro's program repeated the design from her invitation on the lavender cover, and included her name and birth date. Inside the five-page program, printed in Spanish, was

- The name and address of the church
- The date of the celebration
- The time of the mass
- The celebrant
- The musician
- The names of her parents
- The names of her grandparents, including her late paternal grandmother
- The name of the caballero de honor
- The name of the dama de honor
- The names of the flower girls
- The church service, including the music, the lyrics to all songs; the biblical readings, their citations, and the name of the person who read them; the gifts blessed during the mass and the name of the person who presented them.

The program not only tells the guests who is participating and what they did, but serves as a souvenir of the celebration they shared with you.

If the invitation is very detailed, a simple sheet or card that outlines the ceremony for the guests is enough. But if the invitation is simple and you are not having a church service, then you may want to have a program for the reception. You may want to include:

- The name of the quinceañera
- The name of her parents
- The name of her grandparents
- The names of the court of honor
- The date
- The place and address
- Name of the master of ceremonies
- The name of choreographer

- The band or disc jockey or both
- The names of the musical pieces that are part of your presentation and who danced them
- If you are including the crown and the changing of the shoes, who crowned you and changed your shoes
- The theme
- The menu
- The table decorations
- The set designer
- Any other details you want to add or delete to make the night memorable for you and your guests

In either case, the program need not be more than something typed and photocopied, folded in half and stapled into a booklet. Your imagination and your budget are your only limitations.

- Menu cards. For a very formal celebration when you aren't including a menu in a program for the reception or you aren't having a reception program, you may want to have cards printed with the menu at each place setting. You could even have the menu printed on ribbons and laid on the table between each setting, as a decoration and memento for the guests.

The more formal and elaborate the celebration, the more stationery you will need from the printer or bridal shop. If you are having a simple celebration, you really need only the invitations, but even those do not necessarily have to be printed. Blanca Argueta of Bay Shore, New York, wrote her invitations out by hand. A pretty drawing of la quinceañera wearing Blanca's colors—pink and white—graced the front of the invitations, which she found in a party store near her home. Inside, Blanca filled in the date, time, and place of her celebration.

Engraving vs. Thermography vs. Printing

Engraving requires the words to be etched, either by hand (the most expensive) or by machine (less expensive), into a copper plate. The depression is filled with ink, which the paper picks up. The result is very clear, raised lettering. Because the little letter-puddles of ink took time to dry, the printer laid a piece of tissue over the paper so the ink would not smudge. Engraving is very expensive, but it does produce a characteristic indentation on the back of the paper. That indentation distinguishes even the worst engraving from the best, but much less expensive, thermography.

Thermography or raised lettering also gives you something to run your finger over, but is really offset or letterpress printing. A clear resin powder is applied to the printing, giving it a raised appearance, but also blurring the print the tiniest bit. Thermography is more expensive than regular printing, but close to half of what engraving costs. And only the most discerning eye, or finger, can tell the difference. If you are having a formal celebration, engraving is preferred, but thermography is acceptable, whichever your budget allows.

Printing, when done well, makes the fanciest typefaces come to life, especially when a colored ink is used. It is, however, less formal, but also the kindest to your budget.

Finding a Printer to Keep Costs Low

Printing is a highly competitive business, so shop around for the best prices. Once you have decided which stationery items you need, write them down in your notebook of dreams. That way you will know exactly what you want to buy from the printer.

About a dozen companies in this country print social invitations. Chances are the printer you will deal with will take your order and send it off to the company to fill. Some of those companies, like Rexcraft, offer mail-order sales direct to the consumer. You will save money, especially if you want your invitations printed in English. For Spanish or bilingual printing, you may save money by going to a local Spanish-language printer.

If you plan to shop for your quinceañera items at the border, ordering your invitations there can result in dramatic savings. At La Cucaracha, a store in Reynosa, Tamaulipas, that specializes in all the trappings for quinceañeras and brides, there is a nice selection of invitations for a very low price. For less than 500 pesos, about 16¢ at the 1996 exchange rate of 3,000 pesos to the dollar, you can get a hundred invitations. Invitations in the States side run about $1.50 each.

While Anglo etiquette requires a separate invitation for anyone over eighteen, in Latino cultures one invitation serves for everyone living in one household, no matter how old they are. By observing the Latino custom you'll cut down on the number of invitations you have to order.

The invitations to the quinceañera's friends don't have to be as elaborate as the ones you send to the family. You might want to have the invitation wording printed on a single sheet of card stock, which ·can double as an admission card. That way the quinceañera's friends can attend just the dance, rather than having to sit through dinner.

The invitations for less formal celebrations and for the thank-you scrolls, the list of padrinos, the church and reception programs, can all be done on a computer. Desktop publishing programs often come with appropriate art for the cover and a large variety of typefaces to create a look to complement the invitations.

The Personal Element: Designing Your Invitations

Invitation designs are endless—some are laser cut, some are embossed with pearlized inks. Some are imported, some are adaptations of wedding invitations. Some have a young girl on the front or the quinceañera and her court, others are more floral or Victorian. Some are shaped like fans, which are folded and slipped into their envelopes; others bear the Roman numeral XV on the front. Still others have the quinceañera's name or even a picture or two—a baby picture and her quinceañera portrait. The design of your invitation should reflect and carry through your theme and color scheme: carousel horses, roses, fans, a particular fairy tale. It serves as a preview for your guests, a hint of the magical night to come.

When the family and friends of Teresita Perez pulled the creamy invitation from its envelope, they got the first glimpse of what was in store for them. On the invitation was a white carousel horse, with light pink and blue tack decorated with pink roses, pink and blue ribbons flying from its pole. Embossed in gold on the right corner was Teresita's name.

Invitations with pictures of the quinceañera—one of her as a tiny child and another of her formal quinceañera portrait—are also popular. Celia Hernandez had her younger picture on the front and her portrait inside, opposite the wording. Felicia Aguirre had her portrait framed in an embossed heart on the front of the invitation, and her baby picture on the inside.

For something more unique, an artistic friend or the quinceañera herself may want to design the invitation especially for the special celebration. A handwritten note on pastel paper can be quite charming and is always appropriate.

The Wording

How you word your invitations depends on your cultural and family background: sometimes the girl's parents extend the invitation, as the hosts who are presenting their daughter to society; sometimes the girl and her parents extend the invitation; sometimes the girl herself.

Teresita Perez extended this invitation to her guests:

Tengo el gusto de invitarles
a la celebración de mis Quince Años
que me ofrecerán mis padres
el sábado dos de diciembre
de mil novecientos noventa y cinco
a las ocho de la noche
en el Tropigala Banquet Hall
10550 Northwest 77th Court
Hialeah Gardens, Florida
Traje Formal   Les espero
Teresita

I have the pleasure of inviting you
to the celebration of my Fifteenth Birthday
that my parents will have for me
on Saturday the second of December
nineteen hundred ninety-five
at eight in the evening
in the Tropigala Banquet Hall
10550 Northwest 77th Court
Hialeah Gardens, Florida
Formal attire   I await you
Teresita

Giving thanks is a theme that runs through all quinceañera celebrations, whether in a full church service or speeches at the reception by the parents and the quinceañera herself.

In San Antonio, the message of thanks, written by the quinceañera, is frequently part of the invitation.

I, Dominique Estell Chavez,
would like to give thanks in a very special and loving way
to our Lord and the most important people
in my life, my parents,
Mr. and Mrs. Gilbert Chavez.
As I leave behind my childhood years with happy memories
and will be looking forward to my future and happiness,
I would like to extend my love and appreciation to my family,
who have guided me through fifteen years
of my life and who will guide me in years to come.
And to my Sponsors, Court of Honor and Friends
that have made this dream come true.
I would like to cordially invite you to participate

in the celebrating of my Fifteenth Birthday Mass
on Saturday, the thirteenth of May,
nineteen hundred and ninety-five
at two o'clock in the afternoon
Hosanna Lutheran Church
6925 Crestway Drive
San Antonio, Texas

On the left side were details about the time: Reception 6:00 to 7:00 P.M.; Mariachis: 6:00 to 7:00 P.M.; Dance 8:00 to 12 midnight.

On the right was the name of the band that would play that night, and the name and address of the banquet hall: Music by Losoya Band; Plaza Del Rey Ballroom, 2716 Fredericksburg Road.

Formal wording is always appropriate for a formal celebration:

Mr. and Mrs. Richard Gutierrez
request the honour of your presence
at a
Mass of Thanksgiving
given in honor of their daughter
Yolanda
on her
Fifteenth Birthday
on Sunday the thirty-first of October
nineteen hundred and seventy-six
at four o'clock in the afternoon
Incarnate Word High School Chapel
727 E. Hildebrand
San Antonio, Texas

Reception immediately
following ceremony
Villita Assembly Hall
401 Villita

If a church service is not being held, the formal wording is simply changed by substituting "celebration" or "dinner and dance" for "Mass of Thanksgiving."

This wording is popular in Chicago:

Con la ilusión del ayer, la firmeza de hoy,
la esperanza del mañana, doy gracias a Dios
por permitirme haber llegado a mis XV Años, Yo:
[nombre de la quinceañera]
En compañia de mis Padres:
[nombres de los padres]
Deseamos que nos acompañen a elevar una oración
por el Décimoquinto Aniversario en la
Misa de Acción de Gracias
que se celebrará el [día y fecha]
a las [hora]
en la Iglesia [nombre de la iglesia]
[dirección de la iglesia]

With the illusion of yesterday, the fortitude of today,
the hope of tomorrow, I give thanks to God
for allowing me to have reached my Fifteenth Year, I
[name of the quinceañera]
in company with my Parents
[names of the parents]
We would like you to join us in offering a prayer
for the Fifteenth Birthday at a

Thanksgiving Mass
that will be celebrated [day and date]
at [time]
in [name of the church]
[address of the church]

Printers who are familiar with quinceañera celebrations will often offer several wording choices to go with invitations designed especially for quinceañeras for a set price. You can write your own wording, but many times printers don't like to take those jobs. They cost the same to the consumer, but they mean more typesetting for the printer. For those printers not familiar with the celebration, including mail-order houses, you have to supply your own wording.

Spanish or English?

The choice is yours, depending on the language with which your family is most comfortable. Spanish is another legacy of our heritage, and even in families where English is spoken in the home, the invitations are often written in Spanish. To appeal to everyone, bilingual invitations might be printed with each language on a facing page.

Unless you go to a printing company that specializes in Spanish, expect to pay extra. Foreign language charges start at $6.50, usually per order, but not always. In addition, some invitation companies tack on an extra charge for *each* accent mark in the copy, starting at 75 cents—in effect, charging you twice. Other companies do not charge an accent fee, but do charge a separate foreign language fee for each item, such as the invitation, the reception card, and the response card. Sometimes printers, bridal shops, or party coordinators will absorb those fees if you order a package from them. Be sure to ask.

Typing the copy, rather than writing it out by hand, and clearly marking the accents will reduce the opportunity for errors from the typesetter. Make sure the copy you give the printer is correctly spelled and punctuated, including the names and addresses.

Some printers provide proofs of your order for an additional charge. Proofs let you see what the invitations and enclosures will look like and make sure everything is included and spelled correctly. Just make sure that if you order the proof, the responsibility for catching errors does not shift from the printer to you.

Newspaper Announcements

Invitations will let your personal world know about your celebration, but why stop there? Many Latino newspapers and magazines have social pages, and quinceañera celebrations figure prominently. The editors of those publications are often happy to print your picture and an announcement of your celebration.

Sometimes photographers have arrangements to send or at least notify a publication's editor of an upcoming quinceañera when they shoot the girl's portrait. Check with your photographer to see if he or she is one of them.

One to two months before your celebration, call the local paper to find out what their requirements are. They'll often send you a form to fill out, asking for your name, your parents' names, and the names of the court of honor and padrinos. The form also asks what school you attend and what grade you're in. Some publications want a description of your dress and the decorations, and some want to know the menu at dinner. The form may have places for the name of the church and the name of the priest or minister who conducted the service; where your reception was held; the name of the master of ceremonies; the name of the band; the name of the person who baked and decorated the cake; and other details.

Some Spanish-language newspapers and magazines will accept only those narratives written in Spanish. Call the newspapers and magazines directly for their deadlines and their copy and photo requirements as well as the name of the person to whom the information should be sent.

Can't find the address or telephone number of the local paper? Call your favorite local Latino radio station. They often announce their phone number so you can call in requests. Sometimes they even make announcements of quinceañeras and dedicate a song to the honoree during evening programming, a special touch on a special day.

Chapter Twelve ༅

The Bloom of Youth: Flowers, Favors, Decorations, and Transportation

We tried to keep it as simple as possible. You can go into the flower shop and you want everything—it's all so beautiful!

—*Rita Aguirre, who selected the decorations with her daughter, Felicia*

Before her daughter's quinceañera, Norma Garcia of Manhattan spent her evenings and weekends sewing, gluing, stitching, and fitting. "You make everything at home, and everything is color coordinated. I made the centerpieces. I made the souvenirs also. The wineglasses I decorated myself with pearls, and lace. I was sewing for months."

The decorations and favors are what pull your theme together, convey the idea to your guests, and conjure memories of your celebration when they see the favor they have taken home. Your personality is reflected in your favors, and is a little bit of the party, a little bit of the magic the guests can take home to spark their memories of the good time they had.

Even if you are all thumbs or do not have the time to make your decorations, there are myriad sources to find what you need, from high school continuing education classes to craft shops, from party stores to traditional florists.

Garcia gets her ideas from bridal shops. "They have all these souvenirs and you get

FACING PAGES: *The quinceañera cake is a decoration that's good enough to eat. Many are also engineering marvels to rival any structure in the real world. Baker Craft makes this cake, called Juventud Encantada, available through independent bakeries and supermarket bakery departments.* —Courtesy of Bakery Craft

ideas. I buy all the supplies I need from them or from another store and I do them at home. It's cheaper and they come out much better. I put a lot of love in producing them."

One of the best sources of ideas is other quinceañeras. People see what's at other parties and add what they like themselves and what they've seen in the stores. There are small bouquets of helium-filled balloons and Mylar sandbags to weigh them down to decorate the tables. Craft and party stores are a treasure trove of tulle, ribbon, flowers of all types, colors and sizes, medallions, and forms to decorate, such as shoes, baskets, boxes, cups, and glasses. With a little imagination, they can be combined to emphasize your theme, your colors, and your taste to the delight of your guests. You are limited only by your budget and your imagination in creating decorations and favors your guests will want to keep forever.

As you shop around for favors and decorations, jot down your ideas—what you see and where you've seen it—in your notebook of dreams. It's a good place not only to keep samples of the materials that you could use but also to sketch your ideas. When it comes time to buy the materials or order what you want, you'll know where you saw what you wanted and how it fits into your budget.

Everyone Helps

For five months before Octaviana Salazar's quinceañera, her mother worked on the decorations in San Antonio while her aunts worked on them in Laredo, Texas. "My two sisters and a friend, we made the decorations and the glasses for the *brindis* [toast]," said María Salazar. That came to twenty-eight champagne glasses hand-painted with pink roses. There were also forty baskets to trim with pink ruffles and lace and pearls and ribbon, as well as the wrist corsages and the headpieces to make for the damas. Even the cake knife and server were decorated with pink ribbon streamers. Family arrived at the Salazar home two days before the party "to finish everything," María Salazar said.

Many times, when a family announces they are planning a quinceañera for their daughter, the extended family gears up to help. The sisters, cousins, and aunts in the Garcia family each did what she could to make the many touches that make each quinceañera unique—cousins in Puerto Rico sent crocheted fans that Garcia would decorate and turn into capias. Other members of the family brought *cerámicas*, small ceramic items that are traditionally given to guests at Puerto Rican quinces. Each member of the family has a job—decorating, trimming, sewing, cooking, whatever needs doing.

You will probably have plenty of help making the decorations and favors, but you have to give the people working with you an idea of what you want and listen to the suggestions they make as well. If you like their ideas, you may ask them to carry them out. One of your aunts may want to make your capias, another may volunteer to make the net bags of mints and almonds. Your older cousin may have a talent for arranging flowers and may volunteer to make the centerpieces for each table. Perhaps you'll all get together to make potpourri sachet bags, each to be tied with a thin satin ribbon to a folding fan as favors for the women, or to write your name in gold on ceramic boxes that will hold a few chocolates for the men.

Although Laura Valenzuela held her quinceañera reception at a hall that included floral arrangements on all the tables, she and her mother made all the favors that they gave to their guests. Her mother shaped 250 rosaries from *migajón de pan*, a claylike material made from white bread. These were presented in baskets embroidered with pink and white yarn, which Laura was in charge of making. Everywhere they went, they took the baskets and the yarn to work on; when they went visiting, said Laura, they enlisted the help of whoever was there. "We'd all sit there and do them—my grandmother, my aunt," Laura said.

Her mother, Ana Maria, was seldom seen during the months before Laura's celebration without the tote bag of materials she would transform into favors and decorations. "Wherever I used to go, I'd carry my bag with my material," said Ana Maria Valenzuela. "My mother would say, 'Can you leave that alone? Just put it aside.' I'd say, 'No, Ma, I have to finish. I have to do 250. I have to do 300.' I always would concentrate on that."

Flowers All Around

Whether they are silk or fresh, flowers have a special and prominent place at the quinceañera celebration as a symbol of youth and beauty. The quinceañera herself may carry a bouquet into the religious service if she is having one. There are corsages for her mother and grandmothers; boutonnieres for her father, her grandfathers, and the chambelán de honor; wrist corsages or small bouquets for the damas, and even flowers on their headpieces—small combs to tuck into their hair.

You may also want to order corsages or boutonnieres for any and all padrinos. Often they are made of silk flowers or *migajón de pan* or *porcelana,* a kind of dough that can be shaped and colored and that quickly hardens, with the idea that the padrinos can keep them as special thank-you gifts for their support and participation.

Make a list of who you want to carry or wear flowers, whether the flowers will be fresh or silk, and whether someone in the family plans to make them for you or whether you need to order them from a florist.

While fresh flowers are beautiful, they can be expensive and perishable. Many people today use silk flowers, which can be arranged more easily and will keep forever. Silk flowers can be more economical as well. You can buy a silk rose in a craft shop, for example, in whatever stage of bloom you want from a tight bud to a fully opened flower for less than $2. Prices for fresh roses from a wholesaler may *start* at $2 each. You can buy silk flowers a few at a time and work on the table arrangements, for example, over a period of months. Fresh flowers you have to buy the night before and make all the arrangements *that night* with a lot of people to help you. You'll find a list of specific flowers traditionally associated with a birth month on page 20.

The Virgin's Bouquet

During a Catholic mass, the quinceañera customarily places a bouquet of fresh red roses on the altar of the Virgin Mary, an offering of thanks for watching over and protecting her for the past fifteen years, and a plea for her to continue to do the same for the rest of the quinceañera's life. If roses are beyond your means, however, a bouquet of seasonal blooms—daisies in the summer or poinsettias in the winter—is just as beautiful. It is not, after all, the opulence of the offering, but the sincerity with which it's made that makes the difference.

Decorations

Decorations transform the mundane into the extraordinary. In the church, they reflect a festive, celebratory mood. At the banquet site, they set the tone and the ambiance of your party. If you have a theme, the decorations are the vehicle that transports your guests into your fantasy for the night. Something as simple as garlands of streamers tacked into place with two or three balloons or strings of *papel picado,* sheets of tissue paper with designs cut out, strung over the dance floor let your guests know they're in for a good time. Think about what kinds of decorations you'll want for the church and the banquet site.

THE CHURCH

Many times, the decorations are included in the church fee. Check with the pastor to see whether there are any restrictions on decorating the church. Concepción Aguilar, who makes decorations as well as quinceañera dresses in her Chicago shop, told of one family that spent several hundred dollars on church decorations without checking with the pastor to see what would be permitted. When Aguilar and the family arrived at the church the morning of the quinceañera to decorate, the pastor refused to let them in, saying decorations were not permitted. The church was unadorned for the service and the family had to pay for decorations they could not use.

If you are doing your own church decorations, you may want to consider these touches:

- Flowers for the altar, which are often donated to the church after the service.
- Pew decorations. As Lissette Cruz walked down the aisle at St. Luke's Church in Brentwood, New York, she passed a dozen large bows with a tiny lavender nosegay in the center hanging from every third pew. After the ceremony, the family took them to the hall, where they added festive touches hanging on table corners, on the railing of the dance floor, and the ends of the settee, where Lissette sat while her mother crowned her and changed her shoes for the second time that day. (The first was in church, during the mass.)

- Instead of decorating the pews along the aisle, you can use just two big bows to mark off where the court of honor is to sit.
- A white aisle runner.
- Cast-iron or lattice arches at the beginning of the aisle at the back of the church and at the end, near the altar. The arches can be decorated with ivy, birth-month blooms, or flowers that match the theme colors. They can be fresh, silk, or even paper.

THE RECEPTION SITE

Depending on your theme and your budget, you can decorate as little or as much as you like and can afford. Do you want to create the illusion of a tropical garden? Rent some potted palms and ficus trees for the evening. To make the illusion even more real, hire a set designer to create your fantasy setting with stage flats and entryways. You can spend tens of thousands of dollars on decorations, but several hundred will give you a nicely decorated area that highlights the festivities. This is where a floor plan of the room can help you decide what you will need and what the decorations will look like once they are up. Be sure to visit the location first to see what kinds of touches would enhance the setting and write down your thoughts in the notebook of dreams so you don't forget.

With just a few arches, balloons, peacock chairs and lattice screens, some tulle, some artificial vines, and some tiny white Christmas lights, you can create a magical ambiance for you and your guests. Consider:

- Balloons are a very popular and relatively inexpensive way of decorating a hall. A balloon arch in the theme colors that spans the width of a hall or banquet room is dramatic and festive. You can use it to frame the head table, to serve as an entryway into the room, to add definition and atmosphere to the dance floor. Be conscious, however, of blocking the dance floor or the head table from the view of the guests.
- Three to six Mylar balloons filled with helium, tied with ribbon, and anchored with a Mylar bag filled with sand on each table can substitute for a flower arrangement at an informal reception and are much less expensive. Or if you are putting a champagne bottle on each table for the toast, tie the balloons to the neck of the bottle, below the wire that secures the cork.

- Wrapping streamers, ivy garland, or tulle around any poles in the room. The same materials can be used to drape the edge of the head or cake table, securing the ends at the corners with large bows of the same material or satin ribbon.
- Covering the tables in your theme colors, then sprinkling confetti about to set a festive tone.
- Dressing up the chairs with slipcovers and large bows tied around the backs.
- Wrapping tulle garland around tiny Italian lights. These can be draped around a room, across the front of the head or cake table, or around the peacock chair, to lend a soft, pretty glow.
- Tired of seeing arcs as entries? Try plastic columns wrapped in swirls of tulle and lit from the inside. A bouquet of balloons can even be anchored from the top of the columns.

THE HEAD TABLE AND CAKE TABLE

All tables in the room are decorated, but the most decorated of all are the head table and the cake table. At the head table sit the quinceañera and escort. Depending on the size, she may be joined by her court, her parents, and the padrinos.

Lissette Cruz and her escort were the only two who sat at the head table, decorated in pink and white. Behind them, a wooden lattice screen held tulle swags entwined with ivy and pink ribbons. They sat in white peacock chairs, like thrones, from which they presided over the dinner.

In front of their table, ceramic vases waited in orderly rows to be given to the guests as favors at the end of the night. The cake, a quinceañera on a pedestal wearing a pink frosted gown, sat on a table in front of them, surrounded by fifteen decorated candles.

Celia Hernandez and her chambelán de honor also sat in peacock chairs outlined in white tulle and pink pompom bows. In front of them sat a lace pumpkin coach drawn by four white horses, a quinceañera standing inside, and Celia's quinceañera doll.

The souvenirs for the court and the padrinos—usually dolls or something that reflects the quinceañera's theme and colors—also decorate the head table. Lisa Alfaro gave her padrinos wineglasses trimmed with ribbon and pearls. Inside stood a tiny quinceañera dressed in purple and white, Lisa's colors.

Decorated champagne glasses for the quinceañera and her escort, for the court, and for the padrinos, if you have them, are also on the head table. María Lourdes García de Padilla decorated the ones for her daughter, Fanny, using red and white flowers and feathers. Fanny helped her mother make some of the things, working the glue gun. They also made special capias for the padrinos.

For the court, Mrs. Padilla designed toasting cups that were different from the padrinos glasses. And the flower arrangements, two on each table with a 15 in the center, went to the court and the padrinos at the end of the night, as a way of saying thank-you.

The cake table may also be decorated with swags of tulle and greenery, but the cake should dominate the scene. It may be surrounded by the quinceañera doll with the capias either pinned to her skirt or lying in a basket trimmed with silk flowers, lace and ribbon, the decorated candles to be used in a ceremony before the cake is cut, and the guests' souvenirs.

THE DOLLS

Because dolls represent the quinceañera captured at one of the most perfect moments in her life, they are an immensely popular theme. They can be symbols of childhood, icons that capture the day, souvenirs, or simply decorations. Whether you use dolls as part of your theme depends on you, your cultural background, and where you live.

The quinceañera doll, which is sometimes covered in capias, is a gift from the madrina of the capias at Mexican celebrations or a family friend or relative at Puerto Rican and Central American celebrations. When all the capias are given away, what remains is the quinceañera doll in her dress, which is a copy of the real quinceañera's gown. Sometimes the doll sits on the table in the entryway or on the cake table, but other times the madrina of the capias or whoever gave the doll carries it from table to table, accompanied by another guest. They pin a capia on each of the guests seated at the tables. And when they finish, they put the doll on the cake table. Sometimes it's the quinceañera herself, accompanied by her dama de honor or whoever had the capias made, that goes from table to table, greeting her guests and pinning a capia on them.

In addition to the quinceañera doll, the honoree may also receive a last doll, which in Chicago is a brand-new baby doll, still in the box. But in other parts of the country, the quinceañera doll or another doll in a lacy gown serves as the last doll. It symbolizes the last toy the quinceañera will receive in her childhood.

You may even want a doll to top your cake or have as decorations on the guests' tables. A friend of Laura Valenzuela's mother, Ana Maria, made eleven dolls wearing sequined *china poblanas* for each table. They carried out the *folklórico* theme that Laura had. They were raffled off to the guests with a number beneath the doll and underneath the plate.

At the Sawgrass Mills Mall near Fort Lauderdale, you can have a porcelain doll made to order. Alicia Hernandez, a saleswoman there, said two women recently bought dolls for their daughters' quinceañeras. One woman asked that the doll be on horseback; the other wanted a doll made to look like her daughter, who has red hair.

PHOTO ALBUMS

It can be the official album that will hold the celebration photos or a growing-up album, with pictures of the quinceañera through the years; in either case, decorated photo albums are always prized. They may be trimmed with satin, lace, and pearls, and often feature a portrait of the quinceañera in an oval frame on the cover, often in the quinceañera's theme colors.

The photo album makes a nice addition on the entryway table, especially if you've decided to forgo a large framed photo portrait. The guests can flip through it and see pictures of the quinceañera growing up through the years. The last pages are blanks, of course, so you can add photos of your celebration.

CANDLES

Instead of blowing the candles out on the cake, many times quinceañeras have a candle ceremony as part of their presentation. The color of the candles always coordinates with the theme colors, and often the candle is decorated with lace, pearls, and sometimes flowers. Sometimes the candle itself is carried, but you may prefer a candleholder, which is decorated as well. The decorated candles and holders can double as table decorations for the court or on the cake table.

Lisa Alfaro, whose theme colors were purple and white, wound white lace around purple candles. Small iridescent beads wound around the base secured the lace as well as a spray of dried white baby's breath. Her parents, her sponsors, and her chambelán and dama de honor all carried the lit candles onto the dance floor when their names were announced. Lisa came in last and sat in a chair in the middle of the floor for her presentation. When she had been crowned and her shoes had been changed, she blew out each of the candles and danced her first dance with her father.

Nadia Ali also used candles in her celebration as a way of thanking her mother, her family, and all the special people in her life who had brought her joy and helped her through the rough spots. The pink candles were decorated with white and pink ribbons on a tulle base. Before the ceremony, they were used to decorate the cake table.

Favors

Favors are your gift to your guests, a thank-you they can take home as a memento of the fun they had. Capias are the most common favor the guests receive, but often they are only the beginning. Favors frequently appear as part of the decorations that adorn the place settings at each table, but sometimes they are held on the cake table until the end of the party, when they are given to each of the remaining guests. The favors are almost always either handmade or personalized with touches added by hand. Even the *cerámicas*, the ceramic knickknacks favored by Puerto Ricans and Central Americans, are often personalized for the occasion with the name of the quinceañera and the date in gold or one of the theme colors.

CAPIAS

Because capias are so popular, here are some ideas from quinceañeras around the country:

- At Millie Negrón's quinceañera, the guests received tiny woven palm hats, with a ribbon that said, "*recuerdo de mis 15 años* [souvenir of my birthday] Millie Negrón," and the date.

- Michele Nieto's family found small boutonnieres made of *migajón de pan* in Mexico. They put them on the quinceañera doll, whose hair and dress were styled identically to Michele's. An aunt took the doll from table to table to distribute the capias to the guests.

- Fanny Padilla had four different kinds of capias for her guests. There were fans and hats, crocheted from white thread and stiffened with sugar water, decorated with tiny red glass beads, and fixed with a ribbon bearing Fanny's name and the date of the celebration. Others were made of red and white silk flowers, the iridescent snowflakes that dotted the skirt of her dress, and tied with a bow of the printed ribbon. They were pinned to Fanny's quinceañera doll, who wore a dress identical to hers.

- Laura Valenzuela carried her folklórico theme right through her very popular capias, which were made by a woman who works with Laura's mother with materials the Valenzuelas provided. Laura's grandmother sent the raw

Fans and shoes are popular decorative themes at quinceañera celebrations and are often used as table decorations or for capias, the printed ribbon favors pinned to guests. Ana Maria Valenzuela made the small yarn and lace basket for her daughter Laura's celebration. The rosary she crafted from migajón de pan, a malleable material made from glue and white of baked bread.

—Richard Haro

materials from Mexico—tiny serapes, the miniature earthenware dishes glued as accents on the small straw sombreros. Tied around each hat was a length of ribbon with Laura's name and the date of the quinceañera.

- Norma Garcia's family had the capias for her daughter crocheted in Puerto Rico. They sent the needlework, each one shaped like a fan, to Garcia, who decorated them with ribbons, pearls, and the printed ribbon with her daughter's name and the date of the celebration.

OTHER FAVORS

If you're having a sit-down dinner, the reception site manager will tell you how each place will be set. From there you can decorate each place setting with as many or as few favors as you want. You might want to sketch out a table setting in your book, to help you place the favors in the most decorative and attractive way. You can also keep the favors in a decorated basket or make an arrangement near the cake table and distribute them at the end of the evening, as your guests are leaving. Here are some ideas for favors from quinceañeras around the country:

- Nadia Ali recognized all the special people in her life—her parents and the aunts, uncles, and friends who cooked the food and decorated the hall—with a candle-lighting ceremony. The tapers she used were decorated and became gifts of appreciation to the special people in her life. White lace woven with pink ribbon swirled down the tapers, which were fixed in a Styrofoam base. More lace, tulle, and ribbon covered the base, fixed with a plastic medallion commemorating Nadia's special day.
- Dominique Chavez decorated her guests' tables with a plastic champagne glass with a plastic Cinderella shoe on the base. It sat on a plate with mints mixed with salted nuts.
- At Jacqueline Delao's reception, each guest found two gold almonds wrapped in either white or green tulle and cinched with a ribbon curl. At the center of each table, a gold angel holding a silk rosebud sat on a white satin stand trimmed with lace. A dark green candle stood to the side of the angel, amid a cloud of green tulle decorated with a gold rosebud, a white orange blossom, and a green ribbon curl.
- At Teresita Perez's quinces, each place setting was filled with delights for each guest: a gold carousel horse with chocolates, a white ribbon capia, a potpourri favor Teresita's grandmother made, little plastic horses filled with chocolate raisins.
- Each woman who came to Michele Nieto's quinceañera took home a tiny basket trimmed in pink ribbon and white lace and filled with potpourri. Others were left empty and were also given as gifts. Rolando Nieto's family sent decorated tall pink baskets from Querétaro, his home state in Mexico, one for each table. The Nietos

put a bottle of liquor in each basket for each table. A large basket decorated with white lace and pink ribbons held the smaller potpourri favors.

Hiring a Florist or Decorator

Florists, party stores, planners, party professionals, and seamstresses can all recommend sources for the decorations themselves or where to find the material to make them. Your most reliable sources are family and friends who have given quinceañeras themselves.

Many decorators have florist backgrounds. You may need them to do nothing more than point you in the right direction for suppliers so you can make your own decorations and favors. Or you may want them to bring the theme to life with elaborate designs and lighting—the works!

By the time you meet with the florist or decorator, your notebook of dreams will be chockablock with ideas for favors, decorations, and themes. Talk with him or her about how you envision the reception, and then listen to the suggestions he or she has to make. Talk about the budget you have for the decorations and favors so the florist can better advise you how to get the most for your money.

Many times florists and decorators will offer standard packages to their clients. Ask them to break down the package into individual prices so substitutions, if needed, can be more easily made. Rosemary Garcia, the owner of Plaza Boutique in San Antonio, learned to make favors, corsages, and decorations for quinceañeras from her mother, who works with her in her shop. Garcia makes sure that for the receptions she does, every table has at least one centerpiece and is not only decorated but covered with a ruffled cloth with a liner underneath. They can take care of everything, including the hairpieces for the damas and the beadwork for the quinceañera's pearl headpiece, as well as however much or little decorating you want done. Decorating packages run between $250 and $550.

The "Overlooked" Detail: Transportation

Do not forget the transportation, not only for the quinceañera, but for the court as well. Transportation is more than cars or limousines. It is literally the machinery that keeps the day moving, getting the quinceañera, her escort, and her court of honor from one place to another and ensuring they get where they're supposed to be. It's easy to leave the details of transportation to the individual members of the court. But making the arrangements yourself will assure you that everyone will arrive where they're supposed to be at the same time. One San Antonio family that had a double quinceañera celebration rented a city trolley to take the kids from both courts from the house to the church, on to the reception, and back to the house when the festivities were finished. You may be tempted to rent a Rolls-Royce limousine or at least a stretch, but a white Lincoln rented at a day rate and driven by someone in the family may work just as well and be more economical than a chauffeured limousine.

Carlos Padrino of Padrino Limousines in Miami, who rents everything from a Rolls-Royce Phantom V to a regular six-passenger Cadillac limousine, suggests asking limousine companies what cars they have in their fleet to see what the options are. When more than one car is ordered, some limousine companies will discount the price, either against the total amount or off any cars hired after the first one.

Most limousine companies will ask you to sign a contract that specifies the address the chauffeur is to pick up the client, the time he is to arrive, and what his services are to be. Limousine services generally offer a package based on a number of hours—two hours, for example, to pick up the quinceañera, her parents, and her escort, drive them to the church, wait for the service to end, and then drive them to the reception.

The contract should also specify the make, model, and color of the vehicle you want for that day and what happens if there's a breakdown or something else happens to make the vehicle you wanted unavailable. A deposit of 20 to 50 percent is required, with the remainder due when the driver delivers you to your destination.

A gratuity is given according to the service rendered—10 percent of the bill for an ill-tempered chauffeur who makes the passenger open her own door and drives like a maniac; 20 percent for someone who not only helps the quinceañera and her mother in and out of the car, but is pleasant and generally makes the drive and her arrival at her destination as easy as possible.

If you want a special car from a certain limousine company, plan on reserving it four to six months before the event, just to make sure it's available.

Tips for Hiring Transportation

◆ Visit the limousine company to see what is in the fleet. That way you establish a relationship with the owners/managers.

◆ Is a deposit required? Under what circumstances is it refundable? Is the gratuity included? If you plan to pay by check, some companies require a cashier's check or payment two weeks before the date of hire, so the check will clear.

◆ Make sure that at the very least the cars are equipped with two-way radios and the drivers also have cell phones. That way, if there is an emergency or the driver cannot find you, he or she can call for directions.

◆ Give the driver the exact time the church service and the reception start so he or she can gauge what time he or she will have to pick you up.

◆ If the car and driver are hired for a block of time, what happens if the event runs over? How much is overtime?

◆ If you want to change the address where the chauffeur is to pick you up, let the company know.

◆ Verify your reservation a week before the date of your celebration.

◆ If at all possible pay the balance of the bill the day of the party.

◆ The size of the company is not necessarily an indication of their reliability. Whatever limousine company you decide to go with, check them out. Ask how long they have been in business, and ask for recent references for quinceañeras.

Chapter Thirteen &

The Big Day

But after all, *salió bien* [it went well].

—*Susana Martinez, after her daughter Marisela's quinceañera*

Your months of dreaming and scheming, planning and shopping, comparing prices, making lists, and checking details are over. Now it's time for everything to come together in the way you have dreamed. Your big day is about to begin.

The last month has already been a blur of preparations as you race the calendar, and in the last week the clock, to get everything ready on time. And the less time you have, it seems, the more demands are made on you. There are myriad last-minute details to attend to and family and friends from out of town have arrived, wanting your time and attention. The stress and anxiety of trying to make everything perfect can be overwhelming. Good organization and a sense of humor will help you and your family enjoy this once-in-a-lifetime event. Throughout the months of planning, you've made lists of what needs to be done and who is going to do them, so that coming into the last week, you know what details have to be addressed on what days. The memories you want to have are of the family who came to share your day: how proud your grandmother was when she put the crown on your head, how delicious the chicken and rice was that your

FACING PAGE: *Amalia Hernandez on the day of her celebration, resplendent in her dress and crown.* —Enrique Muñoz Studio

Titi Elena made for all your guests, and how no one wanted to leave because the music kept them on the dance floor.

Although perfection is an ideal, good organization will ensure that the important elements are taken care of in advance, that everything is in place. All you have to do is enjoy the attention and love that will come your way throughout this day.

The Rehearsals

You and your court have practiced the dances for months, but chances are your rehearsals have been outside the hall where the reception will be held. Just to make sure that all the elements fit together, that the choreography works in a larger space, and to give you and members of the court a chance to familiarize yourself with any doorways, steps, stage sets, or other props and structures you haven't practiced with before, the choreographer will schedule a rehearsal at the reception site some time during the week before the celebration.

If you are having a church service, the pastor will schedule a rehearsal a day or two before so that everyone who is doing a reading or adding a special touch to your ceremony is clear about where and when he or she should stand for their part. The rehearsal lets you see the way things look and hear the way they will sound during the ceremony. Rehearsals give the participants confidence, because they have gone through their parts at least once. Just walking through the choreography and the religious service will go a long way to chasing out the jitters, which seem to take up residence among quinceañeras and their mothers the night before the celebration.

Crews Control

If you are doing your own food and decorations, gather crews of people who can help you a day or two before and the day of the celebration. You will need a crew for the decorations, another to help you cook the food, and possibly a third to help you serve it. Start enlisting volunteers a month before, being specific about what kind of help you will need. If you are doing all the cooking, you may want someone to help chop onions, store food, or clean chilies. Or perhaps you would rather have people make specific dishes: the beans, the rice, a potato salad.

Make a list of all the things you will need for serving the meal, and put someone in charge of loading everything into the car: aluminum trays, serving spoons and forks, aluminum foil, pitchers for sodas, plates, cups, and flatware for the guests.

Make another list of all the things you want to take to the hall for decorating, and put someone in charge of each item. Do not forget things like masking tape, scissors, ribbon, string, thumbtacks, and extension cords (for the electrical items you are using). If the caterer or the hall manager is going to decorate, make sure he or she understands how you want the tables to look and find out from him or her when they have to have everything so the room will be ready when you and your guests arrive. Ask someone to go to the reception hall after the church service or an hour or two before the reception is to start, just to make sure everything is the way you want it to be.

When it's time to serve the dinner, make sure you have plenty of aprons on hand, so the people helping you do not worry about soiling their party clothes.

Your crews should know where they are to meet you and at what time. With a checklist for the quinceañera and her court, details are less likely to slip through the cracks. Make a schedule for the day of the celebration, specifying when things are to be done, and distribute the list to the crews, the court, and the family.

Some of the things that should be on the list are:

- The delivery of the bouquets and boutonnieres for the quinceañera, court, and family.
- Hair and makeup appointments for the court, the quinceañera, and her mother.
- Any sandwiches or snacks you plan to serve while the court and family are getting ready.
- The time the court will arrive, who is getting ready at the house with you, and who is meeting you there.

◆ The time the videographer and photographer are coming to the house for candid shots.

◆ Calls to the caterer, musician, baker, and limousine service, if you are using one, to confirm the time and place they are to arrive.

◆ If you are making your own food, decorating the hall, and/or setting up the cake and the bar, write down who is doing what, where they are supposed to be, and at what time.

Be prepared for last-minute changes. Susana Martinez made the hair appointment for herself and la quinceañera, her younger daughter, Marisela, two months before the celebration. She thought they would go in at nine and be home by eleven, the time the photographer and videographer were scheduled to come to the house to take pictures of Marisela getting ready. Then a week before, the hairdresser called to say she had double-booked a wedding on the same day, and the bride did not want anyone else in the shop when she came in.

"I said, 'Well, what am I going to do? It's too late to get another appointment.' She said, 'Don't worry, come early. Can you be here at six?' " Susana recalled.

Marisela's day began at five, when she awoke to get ready for her 6 A.M. hair appointment. Her mother and two members of her court went with her. Susana Martinez then dropped Marisela and her two damas at the house, and went on to the dressmaker to pick up the quinceañera doll. The doll, which was being made in a suburban shop thirty minutes away, was not ready until the last minute, Martinez said.

In Puerto Rico, the court traditionally comes to the quinceañera's house to dress, said Jeanine Peace, who lived there for fifteen years and now works in her sister's bridal shop on Long Island, New York. "Whatever cars they're going in, they'll line up in order," said Jeanine. "Sometimes the boys will go in the same cars, too. They'll go to the church, and from there to the *terraza* or wherever they're going to have the celebration. They all go together."

If you are having a party without a church service, you'll have the morning to take care of last-minute details. But make sure to leave plenty of time in the afternoon for yourself, to do nothing but relax and then get ready. Teresita Perez stopped by the hair salon where the girls in her court were having their hair done to see how they would look, then helped her mother and grandmother set up the banquet hall. From noon on, she had the rest of the day to herself.

At 4 P.M., the makeup artist and hairdresser arrived at Teresita's house to do her makeup and hair. Teresita dressed around seven, and at eight-thirty the Rolls-Royce limousine, a present from her parents, came to pick her up to take her to the salon. She did not get out of the car until her father came to escort her to the stage where she would make her appearance as una señorita, at nine-thirty.

The Day Before

The day of Fanny Padilla's quinceañera, all she had to do was get dressed. "The night before we had everything ready," said María Lourdes García de Padilla, Fanny's mother. "The stockings, the underwear, everything so that in the morning we didn't have to look for anything. All she had to do was have her hair done. Nothing else."

The afternoon before your celebration, make sure you have everything you need while you still have time to get any missing items:

- lingerie
- two pairs of panty hose
- shoes you're wearing to walk out of the house
- crinoline
- dress
- headpiece
- whatever jewelry you're wearing
- gloves or mitts

Marisela Martinez did not sleep very well the night before her party. There was the excitement of many relatives who came in from out of town, the thrill of being the queen for a day, the significance of the passage, and the preceding months of planning, fittings, and rehearsing for this day. It had barely begun before she wanted it to end. "I was nervous, too, because they wanted to take a video of me when I was putting on my makeup. I was really nervous. I just wanted it to be over, already," said Marisela.

The video or still camera can be distracting and heighten the jitters, if you pay attention to it. Ignore the camera as much as you can. It's the photographer's job to capture the poignant moments, the happy moments, the moments where you look your best—without your having to pay attention to the lens. You will look more natural if you just breathe deeply and try to relax.

Teresita Perez advises other quinceañeras that the best way to fight the jitters is to spend some quiet time by yourself, away from the last-minute preparations and commotion. Read or watch television, write in your journal if you keep one. Perez spent most of the day of her celebration relaxing in her room, watching her favorite TV shows.

At Last: Your Quinceañera

Fanny Padilla walked into the church thirty minutes before her mass was to begin, but she was already a half hour late. "That happens when there are so many details," said María Lourdes García de Padilla, Fanny's mother. Here's a timetable to follow to take you through your special day:

- The quinceañera's hair and makeup are done three to four hours before the celebration.
- The quinceañera starts dressing two hours before the celebration. Any members of her court who are dressing at her house arrive with their gowns in hand. The photographer takes candid shots. Whoever is decorating the church begins their work.
- An hour before the church ceremony, the quinceañera arrives at the church, as does her court. Those members of the court who were not at the quinceañera's house earlier pick up their bouquets, wrist corsages, or boutonnieres at the church. The padrinos who are participating in the processional arrive. The photographer takes more shots of them lining up. The minister gives everyone any last-minute instructions.
- The church service starts on time.

- In some areas of the country, there are several hours between the mass and the reception. In the Chicago area, formal portraits of the quinceañera, her family, and her court are customarily shot on the day of the celebration. Everyone goes to the photo studio between the church service and the reception.

- If the grandparents are deceased, some families visit the cemetery between the mass and the reception. Lisa Alfaro, whose paternal grandmother died a few months before Lisa's ceremony, and her family visited her grandmother's grave to pay their respects and bring some flowers.

- If you are decorating the salon yourself, when you and your crew get to hang the streamers and blow up the helium balloons depends on the hall manager. You may be able to do everything the night before, like the Padillas, or you may not be able to put everything up until hours before the reception.

- Arrive at the reception hall an hour or two before the reception is to start, to make sure that everything is set up the way you want it. Make sure there is enough ice for the drinks.

- If you are having live music for the cocktail hour, the musicians should arrive at least thirty to forty-five minutes before the guests to set up. Check any sound system you are using. Check any lights needed for the presentation. The master or mistress of ceremonies should arrive to get ready and make sure everything he or she needs is there and review any last-minute instructions from you.

- If the quinceañera is greeting her guests at the door, she should be waiting for them ten minutes before they are scheduled to arrive. Otherwise, security and a family member should be there to check invitations and greet guests, respectively.

- If the quinceañera is to be presented before dinner, she should arrive backstage an hour before she is to make her debut.

- At the end of the dinner or the cocktail hour, the master of ceremonies asks everyone to take their seats, and the presentation begins.

Ariadna Tanguma's Quinceañera Menudo

My quinceañera was very near and my grandmother decided it was about time that I learned how to cook. She took me to the kitchen and told me that the first thing I was to be taught was how to make my grandfather's favorite food.

6 pounds of tripe, cut in 1-inch pieces
1 gallon of water
2 medium onions, chopped
2 cloves garlic
1 tablespoon salt
½ teaspoon black pepper
2 ancho chilies
1 tablespoon fresh cilantro leaves
7 cups hominy
Lime wedges for garnish

For starters, place the tripe, water, onions, garlic, salt, and pepper in a large kettle and let it simmer over low heat for about two hours, skimming fat as necessary. Next, toast the chilies well. Then slit them open and remove the seeds and veins. Grind them until they are very fine and then add them to the kettle. Add the cilantro and let the stew simmer for about two hours. Add the hominy and cook for another thirty minutes. Serve with lime wedges.

Serves 10 to 12

The Gifts

A quinceañera is a birthday celebration, and what is a birthday without gifts? Whatever the padrinos have sponsored is considered their gift to the quinceañera, but some bring personal gifts as well. Other guests may also bring gifts, whether envelopes or brightly wrapped packages with bright ribbons and bows. Have a table set up near the main table where guests or whoever is greeting the guests can put the gifts when they arrive. Sometimes a wishing well, a mailbox decorated with ribbon and lace, or a box covered in the theme colors with a slit in the top is placed near the head table. Guests can put their envelopes inside.

Any gift that's appropriate for a teen's birthday is appropriate for a quinceañera: clothes, jewelry, the latest tapes or cassettes, portable compact disc players, books—whatever she might be interested in. It's fun to highlight the idea of leaving childhood behind, of moving toward womanhood, by giving her something that highlights her new maturity, something more grown-up—makeup, perfume, or lingerie, for example.

If padrinos are not used, parents often

buy their quinceañeras gifts in addition to the party itself. From her father, Millie Negrón received several pieces of jewelry: a ring embossed with "15 años," a chain with a medal that had the number 15. "And we also gave her a large doll, which is made of porcelain and plays a waltz, and has a large 15 on it," said her mother, Enit Negrón.

Quinceañeras usually do not open their presents at the reception but later that night at home, where the party often continues. Everyone gathers for menudo or mondongo, a tripe stew said to cure hangovers.

In South Texas, especially, the family gathers again the next day at the quinceañera's home. The barbecue is fired up, the disc jockey may return, and another, smaller, more informal celebration with the local family and those who have come from out of town takes place. The gifts are opened then.

Chapter Fourteen ◈

Coming of Age Abroad

> What I told my daughter was, "You are my only child. I'll do as much as I can to make something beautiful for you." We ended up spending a little more for the trips, but it was worth it.
>
> —*Rolando Nieto, whose daughter, Michele, had her celebration in Mexico*

Since she had been ten years old, Michele Nieto dreamed of celebrating her quinceañera in Mexico. "All my family's there," said the Lourdes High School sophomore from Chicago. "I hardly have any family here." At first her parents, Esther and Rolando Nieto, tried to talk her out of it, offering to spend the money on a family trip to Europe instead, Esther Nieto recalled. "But she said, 'No, I can go to Europe when I'm working, when I finish school. But I'm only going to be fifteen once.'" So two years before Michele's celebration, her parents started salting money away and talking about it with family members.

Going back for a quince años celebration is a wonderful opportunity to renew one's culture, but bear in mind the details of the celebration may differ from fiestas in this country. The quinceañera may be consulted as to what she thinks about the details, but the decisions are ultimately made by the adults.

FACING PAGE: *Teresita Perez wanted a cruise to celebrate her quinceañera. Here, she boards* The Fascination *with her parents.* —Courtesy of the Perez family

The celebrations themselves are generally more scaled down, with more emphasis placed on family than in the celebrations here. The extended family is intimately involved in the preparations and plans, largely because they are the ones who are actually visiting the banquet halls, finding the band, reserving the church and attending to the myriad details in the home country, while the quinceañera and her family are back in the States, making their travel plans. The extended family is intimately involved in the preparations, and because the distances are so great, the family here should realize they forfeit absolute control over some of the planning and details.

Here or There?

The relatives we have in our home countries are most often the reason girls return to have their quinceañera celebrations. Sometimes it's easier for our family to pack up and celebrate our coming of age with our grandparents, aunts, uncles, and cousins abroad. Doing so will give you very special memories and a culturally authentic experience, rather than one that has been heavily influenced by American culture.

If most of the family is in the home country and would be unable to attend if the celebration were held in the United States, they may be amenable to helping you hold the celebration where they live. Sherry Blend really wanted a car when she turned sixteen, but her aunt, who lives in Cuernavaca, talked her into a quinceañera instead. "Everyone cooperated to make the fiesta," Sherry said. "We almost didn't know what they were doing. We only had to arrive. It couldn't have been simpler," said Claudia Blend, Sherry's mother.

Unless you make frequent trips to your home country or return for several months, more than likely you will take care of some of the details in the United States and leave the bigger things—the church, the reception site, maybe even the court—to the family members who are helping you make the arrangements. Because of the distance, it's impossible to have the same kind of control over every detail that you would if you had your celebration in the States. Having your celebration abroad is much more of a team effort, with aunts or cousins making selections and decisions about elements that the girl and her mother would normally do. Sometimes the result can be ruffled feathers if the communications among family members is not clear and open.

Because of the strength of the U.S. dollar, you will likely spend less money on the quinceañera celebration itself—the dress, the decorations, the music, the reception site—if you are back in the "old country." But add in the airfare for the quinceañera and her parents, brothers, and sisters, and you can figure on spending almost as much as you would to have her celebration in the States. For instance, the Blends estimated that it cost them $5,000 to have the quinceañera in Cuernavaca, but to have done it the same way in Chicago would have doubled the cost. Still, they could not have had the party in Mexico without family there to help make the arrangements, said Claudia Blend. Her sister knew where to look for the things they would need for a successful celebration, being the mother of four daughters. "They've done more parties than we have," said Claudia, who has considerable experience herself through her craft shop in Chicago.

Involving Your Family

It's never too soon to talk with your family about having a quince años celebration. The sooner you bring up the subject, the sooner you will find out whether family members abroad are enthusiastic enough about the idea to help you make it happen. Organizing a quinceañera from thousands of miles away takes careful planning, a trusted family member in the home country to coordinate the details, and plenty of time to work out the logistics.

The more you talk with your family about what you want, the better idea they will have of what you need from them and the better understanding you will have of what is possible and what is not. Sometimes we take simple things for granted—balloons, for example. Here balloons are an inexpensive way to decorate the reception site. But in some parts of Latin America, they can be very expensive. A balloon arch at the reception or church can be more expensive than renting one made of iron, for example. The family member helping you organize will be able to tell you what is realistic and what isn't, what you may have to bring with you if it's something you can't live without.

Cuban Fiestas de Quince *as They Were*

These were simple affairs held in the home, with plans made by mothers and grandmothers months and months in advance. What would her dress look like? What would they serve at the buffet dinner? Who would they get to play the music? Who would they invite? The long gown itself symbolized the girl was on the cusp of womanhood, much in the same way that British boys of a certain age are allowed to wear long pants rather than shorts and stockings. There was no fancy choreography for the court of honor. When the dinner was finished, the quinceañera's father simply led his daughter to the dance floor, the band struck up a waltz and they danced her first dance as una señorita. Nestor Baguer, a reporter for the Cuban Independent Press Agency, recalls attending many such celebrations in his youth.

If you return home on an annual or more frequent basis, one of your trips would be a good place to begin your inquiries. Start with the church and banquet halls. Take whoever is going to help you along, and visit as many places as you can. Talk with your family members and their extended family members for ideas on locations, choreographers, and potential damas or chambelanes. Look at invitations and shop the markets to see if there is anything available you might want to use for decorations or favors. Ask about details we normally do not include in quince años celebrations here—car decorations or decorations for the church doors, for example. The more general information you have, the more ideas you will get and the easier it will be to organize your celebration.

Quinceañera celebrations are studies in cooperation no matter where they are held, but all the more so when the celebration is to be held overseas. The key to a successful celebration outside the United States is to have a trusted family member who will act as your eyes and ears, who will act on your behalf to check churches and reception sites, find a choreographer, find a baker for the cake, and take care of the myriad details. Still, emotions may rise. Susana Martinez's older daughter, Julie, had her quinceañera in Mexico. Her aunt, Julie's father's sister, made most of the arrangements because the Martinezes live in Chicago. "I felt a little left out," said Susana Martinez. "They decided everything." In the end, everything worked out fine. Julie's uncle had a salon, so he took care of the reception site. Another uncle is a musician, so he took care of the music. "It was nice, because we had a lot of help," Susana Martinez said. "For that, I'm grateful. Everyone had a good time, and that's what counts."

Because of the logistics, most of the arrangements will be made by the person coordinating with you in your home country. "Since you can't be there, you can't see how things are, you can only tell them how you want things, more or less, and put them in charge of organizing it," said Claudia Blend. Frequent phone calls to coordinate with your organizer will keep you up to speed on what he or she has found and is recommending.

As you talk with whoever is organizing the event for you about how the arrangements are going, keep lists of things you think of to discuss with your right-hand woman and encourage her to do the same.

Bringing Items from the United States

You may want to bring items for the celebration with you on the plane. Generally, things that are unavailable in the home country, favors you have made yourself or have had made, or the quinceañera's dress, doll, and/or any specially made clothes for members of the family are brought along. Check with customs officials in your home country to find out what you are permitted to bring in and whether there are limits on its value. Lourdes Montalvo began buying tiny Swarofsky crystal pieces that she would give as favors to the guests who would attend her daughter's quinceañera in Caracas, Venezuela. Often the girls have their dresses made here and then carry them on the airplane, or even have them shipped. Paulette Peace made and shipped a dress for one of her clients who returned to the Dominican Republic for her celebration. Esther Nieto packed the fountain for the baker to set up beneath the cake, with its columns and bridges and tiny sugar dolls made by a friend of the family.

The Blends brought with them the dress, the souvenirs, the bouquet, and the crown. Everything else the family in Mexico arranged, including the invitations. Sherry's aunt even picked the court, following the local custom, which is to have all boys in the court. Because she had no close cousins her age, her aunt found four boys from the neighborhood who were Sherry's age; they became her court. From visits to Mexico throughout her life, Sherry had known most of the chambelanes since she was a small child. One was a distant cousin, another lived across the street. Yet another was a cousin of a cousin.

The Nietos relied on Esther Nieto's brother for the preliminary arrangements. He found the church, the choreographer, a florist in the market, and a salon that offered a package that included a sit-down dinner, the disc jockey and band, the videographer and the decorations, even lighting effects for the after-dinner dance. Having family in Puebla to help in the planning and make the arrangements was crucial to the celebration's success, said the Nietos. "We couldn't have done it without them," said Rolando Nieto.

Choosing a Date

Although quinceañeras are traditionally held on or as close to the girl's birthday as possible, many families wait until summer vacation to hold the celebration if they are planning to return to the home country. That way the quinceañera herself can come down two to four weeks before her celebration for the final preparations, including the choreography, buying and fitting the dress there, if those are your plans, and so on. After the celebration, the branch of the family that lives in the States is free to stay for several more weeks, without the constraint of other children in the family missing school.

You do not have to have a specific date in mind when you first begin planning a celebration overseas, especially if you begin planning several years in advance. The person working with you in your country of origin should tell you how quickly facilities book up and when you have to make a firm decision on a date. She or he will know what dates are available for the church and the reception site, if you are not having the reception in a private home.

Having your celebration abroad brings a third element into the picture—airline availability. As soon as you have a firm date for the celebration, remember to call the airline to make reservations for everyone in the family in the States who will attend.

Meanwhile, Back in the States . . .

While your family in your country of origin is scurrying around finding the elements for a perfect celebration, you are not sitting idly by. In a notebook, keep track of all the things you want to talk about with the people helping you and all the details they have for you. Make a list of what you have to find and bring from the States. This may include:

- The quinceañera's attire, including headpiece or crown, lingerie, shoes, panty hose
- Whatever makeup she will need
- The attire for the parents. Unless the quinceañera's father owns his own tuxedo or there is a formal-wear shop in the country of origin that will rent tuxedos, the quinceañera's father usually wears a dark suit or a long-sleeved guayabera over dark trousers.
- The quinceañera doll, which traditionally is a replica of the quinceañera herself, made by the same dressmaker who made her dress.
- The favors, because they are personal thank-yous and souvenirs from the celebration, are often made in the States and carried to the other country. Of course if you find something in the market once you go abroad, you may decide to treat your guests to two favors.
- Any special items that you want to have that are unavailable in the country you are visiting, such as cake fountains, columns and bridges, or a certain song or songs for your choreography.
- A special gift for each of the family members who worked to make your celebration come true. A silver key ring for an uncle, perhaps, or a pin or other piece of jewelry for your aunt or grandmother—something to let them know how much their efforts meant to you.

Quinces in Nicaragua

Historians say the quinceañera tradition arrived here with the Spaniards, but became more popular in the nineteenth century.

Nicaraguan girls traditionally celebrate their more grown-up status during the day, rather than at night. In the late morning, the girl gets ready and puts on a fluffy pink dress. On her father's arm, she leaves the house and walks to church, the rest of her immediate family, her court and her relatives following behind, in a procession.

After the mass, the guests gather at the family's house for a traditional dinner of *arroz con pollo* (chicken and rice) that the girl's mother has specially prepared for her. A local band will play at the dance that follows. The girl must dance with her father first before she can dance with her male friends who have come to celebrate her special day.

While the celebration in the smaller cities and villages is more traditional, in Managua, the parties are held in dance clubs or ballrooms, and traditional Nicaraguan music is replaced by pop American music.

But whether the celebration is held in the city or the country, the cake always draws almost as much attention as the quinceañera herself. The taller, the more tiers, the more lights, fountains, flowers, bridges, the better.

The Final Arrangements

If you can spare the time, it's a good idea to get into town two to three weeks before the celebration to tie up any remaining loose ends, such as finalizing the menu, hiring a florist to decorate the church, finding a hairdresser for the quinceañera, her mother, and any other women in the family, and hiring the photographer.

Over the telephone you refine and hone the list of things that need to be done. From that list, you will know exactly what will need your attention during the two weeks leading to the celebration. Here's a generalized checklist to help you make sure everything is in place.

* The church. Is a meeting with the pastor required for spiritual preparation? When can the florist come in to decorate? When is the rehearsal and who must be there? Have all the readings and readers been selected? Has the music been chosen?
* Reception site. Is the menu finalized? Does it include the cake? If you have ordered a package of services, run through them one last time with the

owner or manager just to make sure everything is set and clear. Also, check with the choreographer to see if there is anything special he or she needs—a tape deck, a microphone, special lighting—then double-check with the reception site manager to make sure those things will be provided.

- The court of honor. Do the people in the court of honor know where they are supposed to be and when? Do they have whatever clothing they will need?
- The photographer and videographer. Are they sure where they have to be and when? Review any special shots you want taken.
- Decorations. Confirm with the florist the number of decorations he or she will provide and when they will decorate the church or reception site.

What may be customary at quinceañeras we are used to attending in the States may be extraordinary in our countries of origin. Make no assumptions that just because quinces are held a certain way in the United States that they will follow that pattern all over the world. Any of the professionals you are dealing with can steer you toward what is appropriate and away from what is not. Here are some areas that are handled differently from the way we would do them.

- The Nietos were ready to serve champagne to their guests to toast their daughter, Michele, at her celebration. But when they told the salon owner of their plan, he discouraged them, saying that most people around Puebla preferred a sweeter wine.
- Markets are a way of life in most Latin American countries, and you can often save money by shopping there. Flowers are an especially good buy from the market. Many times the person who rents the market stall can put together arrangements for the church or reception and craft a bouquet for the quinceañera herself.
- While the quinceañera's court is generally made up of couples here, in the home countries, it's usually either all girls or all boys.
- At the receptions throughout Latin America, the quinceañera sits with her family at the head table, not with her escort. The members of the court of honor each sit with their families at tables around the dance floor.

❧ ❧ *In Brazil,* Festa das Debutantes ❧ ❧

The Portuguese nobility brought the tradition of quince años celebrations to Brazil in the early nineteenth century as a way of introducing their young daughters to society. Today, the fifteenth birthday celebration begins with the girl and fourteen of her friends, who participate in a mass celebrating the girl's birthday. The members of the court, all girls, read the Scripture during the service and sing hymns. Around nine o'clock, the party begins. Students from the local military academy escort the girls, who all wear the same dress in the same color worn by the birthday girl. The guests nibble on endless trays of hors d'oeuvres and cocktails while a disc jockey plays pop music.

But at midnight, the honoree leaves the room. A master of ceremonies reads a biography of the girl, highlighting her parents. The important people in her life—best friends, grandparents, teachers who have made a particular impression on her—are called to the center of the room and presented with flowers, a tribute of thanks to them for their influence on the honoree. Then at midnight an elegant young lady wearing a long, sumptuous white dress appears. She is the birthday girl, about to attend her first ball. Her father leads her to the dance floor and whirls her around to a waltz. She then dances with her escort— her boyfriend, her best friend, maybe a brother, or, if her parents are wealthy, a soap opera star hired for the night. The guests dance until three or four in the morning, when they are given small presents as a thank-you and a memento of a special night.

• After the church service, the quinceañera often stays out of sight until her presentation as a young lady. In some Latin American countries, a change of dress that sets her off from her court signals her change in status.

Special Arrangements

Even in our home countries, not everyone comes from the same town or village. For everyone to come may require special arrangements. Rolando Nieto's family lives in the Querétaro village of Tekis, five hours south of Puebla by bus, and they all wanted to celebrate Michele's coming of age. So Rolando and Esther rented a bus to bring the

❦ ❦ *Coming of Age Among the Zapotecs* ❦ ❦

The Zapotecs, who have lived in Oaxaca for thousands of years, involve the entire village to celebrate a girl's quince años, said Tina Bucavales, a folklorist. "They begin with a walking procession to the church, all fifteen couples," said Bucavales, who did her field work among them. After the mass, they would walk back to the quinceañera's house for the party. The girls wore gowns, which middle- or lower-income families would rent. More affluent families would buy them. And like babies and brides, quinceañeras are beautiful by definition. "The idea was that the quinceañera was making a young woman an attractive life," Bucavales said. "An unattractive woman never had a quince."

Nietos to the party. "The bus was filled with forty people," Rolando Nieto said. He rented enough hotel rooms in Puebla for everyone, and because he got a block, he got a special rate. "They didn't have to worry about anything," said Esther Nieto. "It gave them beautiful memories."

❦ ❦ *Meanwhile, Back in the Home Country* ❦ ❦

Because it is her special day, everything for the quinceañera must be special. Outside the United States, transportation is an important detail. In Puerto Rico, the quinceañera and each couple of her court ride in separate cars, forming a miniparade. Often they are all the same—Toyota Land Cruisers, for example, in one of the theme colors. The quinceañera's car is white and is decorated with a flower arrangement or a doll on the hood. The court's cars are decorated with paper flowers and streamers in the theme colors.

In Mexico City, a limousine company offers quinceañeras a motorized pumpkin coach. A fairy godmother is not included.

Chapter Fifteen &

Other Ways to Come of Age

A civilization in which there are many standards offers a possibility of satisfactory adjustment to individuals of many different temperamental types, of diverse gifts and varying interests.

—*Margaret Mead,* Coming of Age in Samoa

In ancient times, initiates to adult society had to declare the role they would fill in the community. AnnaMaria Padilla, an eighteenth-generation Santa Fean, took that tradition very seriously when she turned fifteen several years ago. She thought of her fifteenth birthday as a watershed. It was time to get serious, to put the things of childhood behind her. To begin her journey on the path she would follow through her adult life: music.

"I viewed my quince as an opportunity to ask my community to accept me as one of their musicians," Padilla said. "In asking for them to accept me in this capacity, I really asked that the community allow me to celebrate their lives with them. Each hallmark of life has a sound and a musical expression. To be a town's musician is such a privilege. I am allowed not only to observe the passing of generations, but in a sense, to narrate our culture."

FACING PAGE: *In ancient times, young people made a commitment to their community when they came of age. Instead of having a fancy party, AnnaMaria Padilla of Santa Fe, New Mexico, celebrated her quinceañera by committing herself to a career in music and recorded her first compact disc.* —David Padilla

Instead of a formal, social presentation at fifteen, AnnaMaria went into the recording studio to cut *AnnaMaria,* her first compact disc. The young musician drew from her performance repertoire to record fourteen classical and flamenco guitar pieces.

Before she had turned twenty, Padilla had cast her magical musical spell for such luminaries as Pope John Paul II. She has also set a goal to speak to Latino youth, to help them get the education that will prepare them for the future. Her advice, which she gives in a book published in 1995 entitled *Don't Wait, Graduate!,* encourages Latino youth to pursue home education and correspondence school as alternatives to poor, unproductive, and sometimes dangerous educational settings.

Having a fancy party is only one way to celebrate your coming of age, but it is not the only way. There are as many ways of celebrating a quinces as there are girls. What is important is that the family recognize and acknowledge the new phase of your life, whether it's with a surprise party at home, a study trip abroad, or even a special quinceañera cruise. If a big party does not appeal to you, let your parents know what would. Considering your choices and making decisions about yourself and your future is one way of showing your family you are growing up.

Travel Broadens the Horizons

Delta Villavicencio had always dreamt of going to Europe. When she moved with her family to Danbury, Connecticut, as a tiny child, they were among the first Latinos in the area. With few Latinas her age nearby, the quinceañera was literally a foreign concept, something her mother, the Reverend Juana Villavicencio, had in her native Dominican Republic.

Rather than have a large party to celebrate her coming of age, Delta wanted to take a trip to Europe instead. And that's what she got. Her parents and uncles pitched in and paid for a study trip to Europe sponsored by her high school. Delta went to France, where she improved her French. Her trip to Europe was only half her gift and half her travels that year. Her parents took her to the Dominican Republic, where she visited with family and officially celebrated her birthday by going to a nightclub with her relatives for the first time. Looking back, she would not have changed anything. "I would have remembered a party, but I definitely cherished my time in Europe," she said. "I could say I've *been* there, you know?"

Study trips abroad are a favorite for quinceañeras who eschew the long full dress, the pomp, and the expense for their parents. The experience is often a girl's first test of herself, of her reaction to the world under adult supervision but not her parents' eyes; it's the first time she has pursued an interest that is hers alone, seen a portion of the world on her own. It gives her a new perspective and a chance to find out what she thinks and get a glimpse of who she is.

Achy Obejas, a Cuban journalist who works for the *Chicago Tribune,* grew up in a family that fled Castro's rise to power. They settled in Indiana, where Achy grew up. She knew she did not want a traditional quinceañera celebration, but asked instead for a study trip to Mexico. It was a watershed experience.

For the first time, Achy heard Spanish spoken with a different accent and different vocabulary. And she heard different points of view on Castro and his rule of Cuba. She returned the following year and became even more familiar when she hitchhiked through Mexico with her cousin.

For most travel study organizations, you must be fifteen to participate in their programs. There are at least four umbrella organizations that run programs in more than ninety countries around the world. Programs last as long as a year or as short as a summer. Some also have programs for families, so everyone can go. You'll find them all listed in the Resources section at the end of the book.

A POPULAR ALTERNATIVE—THE CRUISE

More and more quinceañeras are choosing to celebrate their coming of age on board a ship. Tania's, the Chicago restaurant its owner, Elias Sanchez, named after his daughter, has seen many quinceañera celebrations. But when Tania herself turned fifteen, she chose to celebrate with her family on a transatlantic cruise. "Instead of a party, she wanted a complete week on a ship. So that's what we did," said Sanchez. "The whole family went. She asked for only one friend to go with her."

A regular cruise can be booked through any good travel agent. But a handful are starting to specialize in quinceañera cruises, which combine some of the traditional elements on board a ship. Yolanda Martos of Metropolis Travel Group in Miami, started booking quinceañera cruises eight years ago, when her daughter wanted to go on a cruise rather than have a big party for her fifteenth birthday. For less than $600 per person, Martos put together a one-week cruise on board Carnival's Fun Ship, to either the eastern Caribbean or the western Caribbean. At sea, there is a debutante ball, complete with a candlelight ceremony and traditional waltz, two additional private parties, and special party favors.

Martos takes between twenty and forty girls per cruise, and she books three of them during the summer, to avoid conflicts with school schedules. They're popular because the whole family can come—brothers and sisters, aunts, uncles, the grandparents, and even the quinceañera's best friends.

All the family has to do is make the reservations. Included in the package are:
- Invitations to the events
- The choreography
- The cake
- A video for each girl
- A bon voyage party
- A fireworks party

What to bring:
- Your favorite relatives and friends
- A ball gown for the quinceañera
- A tuxedo for the father and the escort, if one is coming, and any male family members who want to wear one instead of a dark suit
- An evening gown for the mother, grandmother, and any female relatives who are attending

Even the clothes are optional, Martos said. Like a fairy godmother, she has a seamstress at the ready to stitch a gown for the quinceañera and can arrange for the tuxedo rental, if needed. The ports of call on the eastern Caribbean cruise include Puerto Rico, Saint Thomas, and Saint Croix. The western Caribbean cruise calls at Cozumel, Grand Cayman, and Ocho Rios in Jamaica.

If you are thinking of a cruise, find out how long the travel agency has booked quinceañera cruises, what boats they book on, how many girls will be presented on the trip, and how many people are part of the party. They should tell you whether port and entry taxes are included, how much time you will spend in each port, and what visas or other documentation is necessary. What kind of deposit is required? What are the conditions under

A Shopping Spree

Organized shopping trips that bring hundreds of thousands of South American shoppers to the stores and malls of South Florida are nothing new. But shopping trips to celebrate a quinceañera are. More and more girls are talking Mami and Papi into handing over the cash they would have spent on an elaborate party so they can spend it on their heart's desire at the mall. "More teenagers are coming because their parents feel it is part of the growing-up process," said Cynthia Turk, the head of Marketplace 2000, a retail consulting firm. And their numbers are considerable, according to Shelley Emling, who wrote about the trend for the Cox News Service. Experts predicted the teen shoppers would boost retail sales 9 percent in Florida during the last holiday season, nearly double the figure they predicted for sales throughout the country

which you can get a refund? Can the travel agent provide you with references from girls who have participated in the past? Be sure to check them, along with the Better Business Bureau to make sure there are no disgruntled customers. These cruises are often scheduled during the summer months, when the girls and their brothers and sisters and friends are out of school. But summer is also hurricane season in the Caribbean. Ask what happens to any fares and fees you have paid if a hurricane occurs.

Something for the Boys

More than fifteen years ago, when Graciela Rodriguez and her husband started planning the quinceañera for their only daughter, they thought their four sons should have something, too. "We looked at it from a religious point of view," said Rodriguez, a San Antonian. "For us, it was an act of thanksgiving. We were giving thanks to God for allowing us to be with each of our sons for fifteen years."

In at least two dioceses in Texas, Fort Worth and San Angelo, celebrations for boys are the policy. But while the Catholic Church would like to encourage quince años celebrations for boys, the service has not been publicized that much and it has not caught on. Father Arturo Perez of Chicago, an expert on popular expressions of faith in the Hispanic community, said some of the things for which parents are thankful apply as much to boys as to girls.

Like quince años celebrations for girls, a beau party, as they are called in South Texas, should reflect the boy who is being honored. Especially when a religious service is part of the celebration, the boy is encouraged to renew his baptismal vows and commit his life to following the teachings of Christ. Some Church officials feel that making that commitment will help boys step aside if violence presents itself.

Rosemary Zuniga just wanted to let her son David know how very much he meant to her. For his fifteenth birthday in 1984, his mother organized a celebration complete with a court of boys and girls, a mass, and a party afterward. "I wanted my son to know he was special," said Rosemary Zuniga, who as one of twelve children, never had a quinceañera herself.

The celebrations the Rodriguezes had for their sons were more simple than the full-blown party they had for their daughter. They carefully chose the Scripture reading for each boy's service to reflect who he was at that point in time and where he wanted his life to take him. He walked into the church flanked by his parents, rather than a girl. There was no court of honor. The decorations in the church hall, where the parties for each of their sons were held, were simple. Her son did not dance the waltz, nor was he presented to society. Rodriguez spent three months to plan each of the boys' celebrations, because they were so much simpler than the one they had for her daughter.

But that does not mean that a celebration for a boy's fifteenth birthday can't be everything a girl's is—and more. Andy Closner of Mercedes, Texas, had a beau party in 1993 that people are still talking about. Closner had no fewer than twenty-nine escorts and twenty-nine damas in his court of honor. The celebration began at noon with a sit-down luncheon for the court and their parents at a private club in McAllen, Texas, where the guests were entertained with live music. Andy had a custom-tailored white tuxedo for his celebration. The church service included a special drama presentation and Andy received a Bible from his father. The reception included four choreographed numbers, including two waltzes, and a fifteen-tier cake that served 1,400 guests.

Debutante Balls and Cotillions

In many places across the country and in Puerto Rico, groups of quinceañeras are presented to society. In Chicago, there is the Cordi-Marian Cotillion. The historical society of Zapata County, Texas, organizes the annual Quinceañera Ball. In El Paso, there is the Symphony Debut. Each has its own requirements, which are often used as a means to ensure the girls are "of good character." The Cordi-Marians, for example, requires each prospective girl to

- have turned fifteen that year
- file a written application in December preceding the cotillion
- bring her parents to an interview with the nuns. The parents must be married to each other. A girl whose parents are divorced is ineligible.
- be chaste
- be respectful of everyone
- miss no more than three weekly rehearsals, which run from the end of January through the cotillion, which is at the end of April

- be punctual
- draw at least half her heritage from Mexico, since the cotillion is designed to preserve the tradition of a Mexican debut
- pay an entry fee of "several hundred dollars," which includes the girl's entrance ticket

Family members must buy additional tickets at fifty dollars each. Still, after the parents pay for the entry, the dress, the escort's tuxedo, the total approaches several thousand dollars, which is still less expensive than a full-blown private celebration.

Requirements are everything for debuts and cotillions, and they vary from event to event. The emphasis can be more on the social aspect—meeting and forming bonds with other girls who have the same ancestral roots, for example, or come from the same social class. There are months spent in rehearsals.

The Hispanic Debutante Association of Fort Worth adds another requirement to their participants: they must be willing to work to raise scholarship funds during the year they are a member at events such as fashion shows. The annual ball, at which the girls are presented to society, takes place in March. At the end of the year, the girls divide up the scholarship pot, handing out amounts that coincide with each girl's participation.

Surprise!

Amneris Rodriguez of Manhattan did not want anything special for her fifteenth birthday, or any other birthday for that matter. "I don't like parties," said Amneris, who lives in New York. Nothing about a formal quinceañera appealed to her. She did not want the dress or the fuss or the attention focused on her on that day. She did not want the pressure of having to be a public princess. Her mother, Nereida Peña, however, had very fond memories of her own celebration and wanted to give her daughter the same kind of quince años party she had had in Santo Domingo: a surprise.

For two months before the party, Nereida Peña made decorations and favors. She planned and plotted how to make arrangements to fete her oldest daughter without her knowledge. She ordered the cake and enlisted the help of Amneris's friends.

On Amneris's birthday, her mother took her to church for a blessing from the parish priest. Then her aunt came from the Bronx to pick her up. She stayed with her aunt overnight, giving her mother a chance to get the apartment ready for the party. Her aunt took her to a beauty salon to have her hair done and then to buy a new dress and shoes. All this preparation and pampering were to go to dinner with four of Amneris's friends, which they were to pick up at Amneris's apartment—or so she thought.

When Amneris walked through the door, she found more than a hundred family and friends, including the godmother she had not seen in eight years, ready to celebrate her fifteenth birthday. "I started crying and my friends were crying and everyone was singing happy birthday. All my family, all my friends, they were hugging me and kissing me," Amneris recalled.

Nereida Peña placed a rhinestone crown on her oldest daughter's head and Amneris's father danced a waltz with her. And for the first time in her life, she did not stop dancing until the party ended near dawn.

Resources 🖎

By themselves, each of these businesses provide key elements for quinceañera celebrations. But for their customers, the owners are invaluable fonts of advice and recommendations on making your celebration all that you want it to be. Many have been in business for a number of years. Many women who used some of these resources for their quince años celebrations turn to them again when their own daughters reach that magic moment.

Banquet Halls and Caterers

Alonso's Escorial
4501 N. 10th
McAllen, TX 78504
210-686-1160
  Caters throughout the Rio Grande Valley.

Angelitos Banquet Hall, Inc.
300 Palm Avenue
Hialeah, FL 33010
305-888-9345
305-888-4979
  Will cater your party and has a pumpkin coach available to rent for your presentation.

Casa Chapala
107 E. Columbia Drive
Kennewick, WA 99336
509-582-7848
e-mail: chapala@cbvcp.com
website: http://www.cbvcp.com
  Off-site catering featuring Mexican specialties or on-site at the Fiestas del Sol banquet hall. Decorations are available.

El Tesoro Party House
3110 Nogalitos
San Antonio, TX 78225-2310
210-532-1345
Joe Duncan, manager
  Brick walls lend a patio atmosphere. You can hire a caterer or bring in your own food.

Garcia Properties, Inc.
2806 Fredericksburg Road
San Antonio, TX 78201
210-737-9407
210-733-3713 (fax)
Diana Sandoval, manager
  Garcia owns and manages six halls in the San Antonio area. You bring in the food.

Logan Square Auditorium
2539 N. Kedzie Boulevard
Chicago, IL 60647-2655
312-252-6179
  Will accommodate several hundred people. The catering is up to you.
Louis's Restaurant

2210 Kerrigan Avenue
Union City, NJ 07087
201-866-1200
Vincent or John Gallotti
  A popular place for quinces.

Park Casino Caterers
572 57th Street
West New York, NJ 07093-1275
201-865-1111
  Just across the river from Manhattan.

Schuetzen Park
3167 Kennedy Boulevard
North Bergen, NJ 07047
201-865-0868
Alicia Huergo or Karl Stuhlmann, managers
  Several rooms and menus to choose from.

Tania's Restaurant
2659 N. Milwaukee Avenue
Chicago, IL 60647
312-235-7120
312-235-7954 (fax)
Elias Sanchez, owner
  A tiled fountain is the center of the beautiful wood-paneled dining room. Elias Sanchez can offer comprehensive party packages that include not only the food, but the decorations, music, and a master of ceremonies.

Cakes

Bakery Craft National
800-543-1673
  National bakery company featured in independent bakeries and supermarket bakery departments, where they offer Juventud Encantada, a quinceañera cake for 260 people. Call them for an outlet nearest you.

Rosario
Bizcocho Dominicano
507 W. 170th Street
New York, NY 10032
212-927-8587
Rosario la biscochera makes light, sweet Dominican cakes as simple or as elaborate as you'd like. You pick your favorite fruit filling.

HEB Grocery Stores
San Antonio, Texas

King Kullen Grocery Company, Inc.
(corporate headquarters)
Prospect Avenue
Westbury, NY 11590
516-333-7100
  Both King Kullen and HEB carry the Bakery Craft line, which includes Juventud Encantada, a quinceañera cake for 260 people.

Marivi's Custom Cakes
By appointment only
305-388-0010
  Trained in Puerto Rico, Marivi Bassabe will make elegant cakes to your taste.

Wally Mejia
Edinburgh, Texas
210-383-1332
  Wally Mejia's cakes are known throughout Texas. Cakes with bridges and fountains aren't his style. But you can't beat him for beading on the cake to match the dress, for intricate frosting patterns, and for sheer elegance.

Original Cakes by Sixta
By appointment only
305-226-6486
  Dominican cakes custom made by Sixta Hernandez. Call for an appointment.

Choreographers

Ballet Folklorico de San Antonio
10 10th Street
San Antonio, TX 78215-1536
210-220-1055

Fidel Hombra
Danbury, CT
203-791-8269

Founder of a Dominican folkloric dance company and expert on Caribbean Latin dance and music. By appointment only.

José Luis Ovalle, artistic director
Mexican Folkloric Dance Company of Chicago
3842 S. Archer Avenue
Chicago, IL 60632-1014
312-254-7521
773-247-1522
Ovalle has a wealth of knowledge about quinceañera waltzes. He can also make his more experienced dancers available for a choreography or as chambelanes.

Rosendo Ramon
By appointment only
305-819-2615
305-839-5031 (beeper)
A Cuban choreographer who tailors the dances to each girl, whether she wants something very traditional or very modern.

Church Services
Quinceañera Guidelines
Roman Catholic Church
Diocese of Phoenix
400 E. Monroe
Phoenix, AZ 85004
602-257-0030

Quince Años: Celebrando un tradición
Celebrating a Tradition, by Sister Angela Erevia, MCDP
San Antonio: The Missionary Catechists of Divine Providence, St. Andrew's Convent
4650 Eldridge Street
San Antonio, TX 78237
210-432-0113
Also available through the Mexican American Cultural Center Bookstore.
3019 W. French
San Antonio, TX 78228
210-732-2156, ext. 104
210-732-9072 (fax)

Rivers of Living Water
by Marie Avilés de Jesús, Roberto Navarro, and José David Rodriguez-Hernández
Frank Klos and Ivis LaRiviere-Mestre, editors
Living Waters of Faith Series
Minneapolis: Publishing House of Evangelical Lutheran Church; Augsburg Publishing House/Fortress Press

Cotillions and Debuts
Cordi-Marian Settlement
1100 South May Street
Chicago, IL 60632
312-666-3787
Sister M. Theresa, MCM

Fiesta en Xochimilco
League of Mexican-American Women
P.O. Box 26522
Tucson, AZ 85726-6522
Alice Eckstrom, president

Hispanic Debutante Association of Fort Worth
P.O. Box 4792
Fort Worth, TX 76164-0792
Tina McCalip, president
817-572-3030

The Quinceañera Ball
Vesta Club
P.O. Box 864
Phoenix, AZ 85007
602-255-0980
Dr. Mary Jo Franco French

Zapata County Historical Commission
P.O. Box 267
Zapata, TX 78076
210-765-4650 (home)
210-765-4822 (office)
Roberto Montes

Decorations and Favors
Balloons Balloons
667 N.W. 124 Avenue

Miami, FL 33182
305-264-6669
  Balloons are just part of what Justo and Xiomara can do to liven up a party. They are also expert disc jockeys and masters of ceremony who will keep your celebration moving.

Crafts by Claudia
4300 S. Archer
Chicago, IL 60632
312-247-4387
Claudia Blend, owner
  An outstanding selection of materials to transform into decorations, favors, and accessories. If you prefer, let Claudia design something especially for your celebration.

Daisy Florist
4923 Bergenline Avenue
West New York, NJ 07093
201-866-4432
  You can also find quinceañera cake tops and decorations, as well as peacock chairs and tables for the party.

El Arte Religioso
4909 Bergenline Avenue
West New York, NJ 07093
201-866-0111
201-865-6255
  They have a full line of invitations, favors, decorations, and dolls. They do their own printing in English as well as in Spanish.

GENY Flowers
4114 Bergenline Avenue
Union City, NJ 07087
201-865-9393
  Fresh flowers, silk flowers, decorations—they're all here.

Gregory's Party Supplies
68 Clinton Street
New York, NY 10002
212-228-8378

212-228-8379
  Gregory's store is chock-full of the materials you'll need to make any decorations and favors you can imagine, or he'll have them made to order.

JB Classic Elegance
480 and 490C E. 4th Avenue
Hialeah, FL 33010
By appointment only
305-884-5400
  Decorations, set and lighting designs, dresses.

Marlene's Exquisite Party Favors
By appointment only
305-261-0504
  Specializing in *porcelanicrón* favors.

Parties by Lizy H.
305-620-0211
By appointment only
  Chocolates and favors, especially designed and made for you.

Party and Bridal Outlet
5640 West Cermak Road
Cicero, IL 60650
708-863-6252
708-863-6275
  Material to make bouquets, decorations, capias, etc.

Plaza Boutique
2720 Fredericksburg Road
San Antonio, TX 78231
210-734-8154
Rosemary Garcia

Special Occasion Engraving
Magical Intricacies—A Custom Engraver
P.O. Box 10196
Spokane, WA 99209
509-465-1606
509-466-7835 (fax)
website: http://members.aol.com/ Engrvd/ engrave3.htm

e-mail: Engrvd@aol.com

Offers cake toppers, engraved toasting flutes, guestbook, and plumed pens. Can order by e-mail or through the website.

Dolls

Art Treasures of Sawgrass Mills
Sawgrass Mills Mall
12801 W. Sunrise Boulevard, #707
Sunrise, FL 33323
954-846-0595
954-846-1132 (fax)

Dress Shops

Alfred Angelo Dreammaker
Manufacturer's Bridal Outlet
Sawgrass Mills Mall
12801 West Sunrise Boulevard
Sunrise, FL 33323
305-846-9198
305-846-8143 (fax)

Azteca Plaza
1010 E. Washington
Phoenix, AZ 85034
602-253-2171

An entire mall devoted to quinceañera and wedding dresses, accessories, decorations—you name it.

Eduardo's
1001 S. 10th Street
Tiffany Plaza
McAllen, TX 78501
210-687-9246

Eduardo's
6941 San Pedro Avenue
San Antonio, TX 78216-6206
210-349-1635

Eduardo's has two locations, one in the Rio Grande Valley, the other in spacious new quarters in San Antonio. Both offer tremendous selections for the quinceañera, her court, and her mother. A nice array of accessories is also available.

Elegant Touch Bridals

733 Suffolk Avenue
Brentwood, NY 11717
516-231-4177

Paulette Peace, the owner, herself was in a quince court. Paulette, her mother, and her sister offer top-notch alterations on ready-to-wear dresses. But if you can't find something on the rack, they'll stitch something especially for you. They also offer a variety of accessories, including lingerie, jewelry, dolls and capias and invitations in Spanish and English.

Melanie's Bridal & Quinceañera Shop
1823 Bingle Road
Houston, TX 77055
713-461-7378

Monte Carlo Studio and Bridal
4506 W. Commerce Street
San Antonio, TX 78237-1628
210-435-1410

Tuxedo Fashions of California
111 Town and Country Village
San Jose, CA 95128
408-249-1269
408-249-1279 (fax)

Randy Solomon offers more than 60 styles of tuxedos. In-store alterations and a mail-in measurement program are available for members of the court or family coming from out-of-town. Quinceañera discounts available.

Dressmakers

Arecia's Creations
3604 New York Avenue
Union City, NJ 07087
201-864-7388

Custom- and ready-made gowns and accessories, including capias and invitations.

Boutique de Novias Nora
Matamoros 596
Reynosa, Tamaulipas, Mexico
22-51-95

They specialize in *los tres Bs—bueno, barato, y bonito*

(good, inexpensive, and pretty), and can make dresses in twelve hours. A selection of bouquets, crowns, and headpieces are available.

Cortes Modernos Aguilar
1708 S. Paulina
Chicago, IL 60608-1917
312-666-5904
Concepción Aguilar specializes in quinceañera dresses, accessories, and decorations, as well as invitations.

Fiesta Azteca
870 Division Avenue
San Antonio, TX 78225-2586
210-924-2717
Owner Maria Ramos can look at three pictures of dresses in a magazine, combine the elements you want from each, and create something unique. She also makes whatever accessories and decorations you may want—headpieces for the quinceañera and her court, dolls, capias, toasting glasses, and whatever else you may need. She will do mail order.

Las Fiestas
Abasolo 6 y 7
No. 608
Matamoros, Tamaulipas 87300, Mexico
12-29-96
16-46-06

Amparo Gonzalez
Chicago, IL
312-254-7521
The costumer for the Mexican-American Folkloric Dance Company of Chicago, who sews exquisite quinceañera gowns as well.

Margie's Photo Studio and Bridal Shop
3822 W. North Avenue
Chicago, IL 60647
773-252-1863
Formerly Benily's Bridal Boutique. The owner, Margie Raices, offers custom-made dresses for the quinceañera and her court, for the damas as well as for the chambelanes. You'll also find a complete line of accessories, right down to the shoes, decorations, and recommendations for choreographers, banquet halls, and just about anything else you'll need, including photos.

Nilda's Bridal
84 Clinton Street
New York, NY 10002
212-387-0460
Gowns, accessories, and decorations, made to order.

Norhill's Bridals
123 S. Broadway
McAllen, TX 78501
210-687-6609
210-687-8854
Ready-made dresses and a large selection of accessories.

Novias Gaby
Matriz: 8a. 126 Abasolo y González
Sucursal: 8a. 1217 Abasolo y González
Matamoros, Tamaulipas 87300, Mexico
13-63-12
Just over the border from Brownsville, Texas, Novias Gaby can make any dress, accessory, or decoration you can dream up.

Dress Shops—Rentals
Gowns to Go
The 840 Plaza
840 E. Oakland Park Boulevard, #101
Fort Lauderdale, FL 33334
954-565-0112

Naomi Bridal and Formal Wear II
100 E. Oakland Park Boulevard
Fort Lauderdale, FL 33334
954-565-0132
Also does invitations, in Spanish or English.

Flowers
Margarita Barrera
2224 S. 29½

McAllen, TX 78503
210-631-5164

The Flower Shop
1622 E. Tyler
Harlingen, TX 78550
210-421-4424
800-736-4124
Greg and Bertha Salazar, the owners, can make fresh or silk flower arrangements for church or reception.

Food
Boriken Bakery
2638 W. Division
Chicago, IL 60622
312-276-1780
Michael Reyes Lopez and Zenaida Lopez offer exquisite appetizers and desserts.

Hair and Makeup
Enit's Hair Design
5951 W. Grand Avenue
Chicago, IL 60639-2739
773-237-1329
A full service salon—hair, nails, makeup.

For Ever
Carmen Castro
718-821-9568
Castro not only does hair, but also manicures, makeup, even facials. She has a line of jewelry.

Invitations
Naomi's Bridal and Formal Wear II
100 E. Oakland Park Boulevard
Fort Lauderdale, FL 33334
954-565-0132
English or Spanish; also rents and sells dresses.

Jewelry
Michael's Jewelers
Oak Plaza
90 E. Oakland Park Boulevard
Fort Lauderdale, FL 33334

305-565-1992
305-565-6534 (fax)
Has a selection of quinces rings and necklaces, some set with stones, in gold or silver.

Music
AnnaMaria
Musica Mundial Productions
P.O. Box 6097
Santa Fe, NM 87502
505-983-6237
Classical and flamenco guitar for the church service or the cocktail and dinner hours.

Paul Elizondo Orchestra
San Antonio, TX 78228-4855
210-433-2012
One of the great society bands of South Texas.

Infinite Legacy Mobile D.J.s
San Francisco Bay area
Mario Ortiz 415-587-2894
Irvin Ortiz 415-586-1067
Fernando Padilla 415-586-4869
e-mail: infinite@inthemix.com
website: http://www.inthemix.com/
Mario and Irvin Ortiz have been in business for more than ten years, providing music for hundreds of quinceañeras. "Big or small, we do them all" is their motto. Lighting and effects are available.

Professional Music Services
Andrés Trujillo, director
305-445-2759
305-210-8667 (beeper)
Trujillo, a violinist, manages the two groups he plays in. He joins his wife, Darlene, who plays piano, for cocktail and dinner hours. As part of the eight-piece Orchestra Almendra, he plays music to dance to.

Rotations On-Line
802 Northridge Drive
Norristown, PA 19403
610-631-1779
610-631-1984 fax
e-mail: rotation@ix.netcom.com

(send to Don)

website: http://www.rotations.com

Their main business is providing CDs to professional DJs, but they also offer compilation CDs for parties, including salsa, merengue, and "Celebrando," a disc that include tracks appropriate for quinceañeras.

Tejano Superstars
210 Palestine Boulevard
San Antonio, TX 78211-1132
210-922-2332

Tejano Music Talent Agency
210 Palestine Boulevard
San Antonio, TX 78211-1132
210-922-9887

Albert Esquival runs both these booking agencies. He can find a band to fit your taste and price range just about anywhere in the country.

Tejas Music Machine
By appointment only.
San Antonio, TX
210-680-0503
Joe "Pepe" Sanchez

Music for everyone—Tejano, conjunto, oldies, country, rap-new wave.

24KT Sound and Video
310-547-4702
e-mail: marc@24ktsound.com
website: http://www.24ktsound.com

Among the several DJs affiliated with 24KT Sound is Nelson, who is bilingual and has a number of years' experience spinning discs at quinceañeras.

Newspapers

You'll find a complete list of Latino publications that print in both English and Spanish, as well as Spanish-language radio stations, in *The Complete Hispanic Media Directory*, published by AR Publications. These are included.

El Heraldo de Broward
1975 E. Sunrise Boulevard
Fort Lauderdale, FL 33304-1433
954-527-0627

The largest circulation Spanish-language weekly in Broward County. Send social announcements to the managing editor.

El Noticiero
2613 Davie Boulevard
Fort Lauderdale, FL 33312
954-792-8019
954-792-2881 (fax)
Eduardo Quiroga, director/publisher

Spanish, biweekly. Social page items due the fifth and twentieth of the month. Copy must be in Spanish.

Party Planners

Parties by Lizy H.
By appointment only
305-620-0211

Lizy also makes favors, decorations, and handmade chocolates and has Birchcraft and Carlson craft invitations in Spanish and English.

Pretty Party
P.O. Box 351526
Miami, FL 33156-1526
305-634-6010
Esther Penton Nodarse

La reina of Cuban quinceañera planners, who can help you organize and coordinate as simple or lavish a celebration as you like. Penton Nodarse also serves as the mistress of ceremonies at the celebration itself.

Photographers and Videographers

Salvador Hernandez
2256 W. 19th Street
Chicago, IL 60608
312-733-6835

Muñoz Studio
664 W. Oakland Park Boulevard
Fort Lauderdale, FL 33311-1728
305-564-7150

Enrique Muñoz Studio
2498 S.W. 8th Street
Miami, FL 33135
305-541-0103

Panorama Photo Studio and Video Productions
5370 Palm Avenue, Suite #3
Hialeah, FL 33012
305-823-5709

Pilsen Photo Studio
1750 W. 18th Street
Chicago, IL 60608
312-666-5442
Arturo Cortes, owner/photographer

Don Polo Video and Photo
3780 Gandalf Drive
Salt Lake City, UT 84118
801-967-9106
Adilfa Ford, owner

Tony's Photo Studio
4911 Bergenline Avenue
West New York, NJ 07093
201-865-4334
　Tony offers more than photos at this shop. Dresses and tuxedos are also available.

Twins Video Productions
Miami, FL
By appointment only
305-826-2614
305-366-9606 (beeper)
Frank Rodriguez
Tony Rodriguez

Transportation
Avanti Limousines
P.O. Box 740167
Houston, TX 77274-0167
713-556-LIMO
713-556-5466
800-TXLIMOS (800-895-4667)
713-266-8581 (fax)

website: http://www.houstonet.com/avanti
　avanti3.html
　Offers 6-, 8-, or 10-passenger stretch limousines or Town Car sedans, uniformed drivers, and a national network of affiliates.

Eagle Carriage Company
By appointment only
516-423-4668
　Sam and Tony Uliano can bring you to the ball in Cinderella style, in a white carriage drawn by a white horse or two.

Padrino Limousine Service, Inc.
4120 N.W. 25th Street
Miami, FL 33142
305-871-6767
305-871-1440 (fax)
　In addition to their fleet of standard and stretch limousines, they also have a Rolls-Royce and a Bentley, if a specialty car is in your fantasy. They can also arrange for just about any kind of transportation you want, from a horse-drawn carriage to a yacht.

Miscellaneous
Jan's Custom Knits
P.O. Box 1197
Hollister, CA 95024
408-637-3269
website: http://www.puffin.com/puffin/
　index.html
　Custom-knit 32-inch by 48-inch personalized blankets in your choice of acrylic, cotton, or wool for a great gift. Features a quinceañera wearing her crown and holding her bouquet and the date of the celebration. Or you can buy the pattern and make the blanket yourself.

The Mexican Fine Arts Museum Center
1852 W. 19th Street
Chicago, IL 60608-2797
312-738-1503
　Has a bookstore chock-full of books and items that can be used for decorations and favors for a folkloric theme.

Travel

ASSE International Student Exchange Programs
12951 Bel-Red Road, Suite 180
Bellevue, WA 98005
206-450-0957
   Study programs available in twenty-four countries in Europe, Mexico, Thailand, and New Zealand. Language training in Spain, France and Germany. Limited scholarships available. Costs range between $2,550 and $6,500.

AYUSA
One Post Street, Seventh Floor
San Francisco, CA 94104
800-727-4540
415-616-0582 (fax)
   Organizes study abroad programs for teens in fourteen areas of the world, ranging from a summer to a year.

EF Institute for Cultural Exchange
One Memorial Drive
Cambridge, MA 02142
617-252-6000
617-494-1389
   Programs enable teens to live with a family abroad and attend a local high school for one semester or an academic year. Programs are available in Australia, Canada, France, Germany, New Zealand, and the United Kingdom.

Metropolis Travel Group
2540 N.W. 29th Avenue
Miami, FL 33142-6438
305-635-1047
Yolanda Martos, owner
   Books quinces cruises to both the eastern and western Caribbean, complete with a debutante ball.

National Registration Center for Study Abroad
(NRCSA)
Box 1393
Milwaukee, WI 53201
414-278-0631
414-271-8884 (fax)

e-mail: inquire@nrcsa.com
   Offers programs in twenty-two countries; programs in Austria, France, Spain, and Canada are specifically designed for teens. Also offers family programs.

World Learning
Kipling Road
P.O. Box 676
Brattleboro, VT 05302-0676
802-257-7751
802-258-3248 (fax)
   A high school program gives students an opportunity to live with families and attend high schools in Europe and Latin America. The Experiment in International Living programs gives high school students three- to five-week programs that include travel, language study, ecological adventure, and community service in Africa, Asia, Australia, Europe, and Latin America.

Youth for Understanding
U.S. National Office
3501 Newark Street NW
Washington, DC 20016
800-833-6243
202-895-1104 (fax)
e-mail: USA@mail.yfu.org
   Study programs available from a few weeks to an academic year in length in thirty-two countries in Europe, Latin America, and Asia. Financial aid available.

Index